WAR TORN SKIES

# BUCKINGHAMSHIRE

*by*

*Paul Johnson*

First published 2014.
Red Kite
PO Box 223,
Walton-on-Thames,
Surrey, KT12 3YQ
England
Tel. 0845 095 0346

© Paul Johnson 2013
All Rights Reserved.
No part of this publication
may be reproduced, stored
in any form of retrieval
system, or transmitted
in any form or by any
means without prior
permission in writing
from the publishers.

Series Editor Simon W Parry.
Design Amy Shore.

Printed by
Dimograf, Sp. Z o. o. Poland
Purchase this and other Red Kite books directly from Red Kite's websites;
www.redkitebooks.co.uk
www.wingleader.co.uk

First Edition
ISBN 978 1 906592 12 7

# CONTENTS

| | |
|---|---|
| **Introduction** | 5 |
| **Aircraft Accident Investigation** | 7 |
| **The Airfields** | 8 |
| **Buckinghamshire Map** | 14 |

**The Golden Years**
| | |
|---|---|
| Stall in a Storm at Ivinghoe | 15 |
| Lysander Discovery at Denham | 18 |

**1940**
| | |
|---|---|
| Formation Flyer Lost at Weston Turville | 20 |

**1941**
| | |
|---|---|
| A Hurricane Hits Bledlow – Death of an ATA Pilot | 22 |

**1942**
| | |
|---|---|
| Summer of Gallant Civilians | 26 |
| "My Dear Val" – The Death of Valentine Henry Baker | 32 |

**1943**
| | |
|---|---|
| George Medal Won at Fawley | 37 |
| A Foggy Night at Mursley Water Tower | 40 |
| A Blazing Wimpey in Winslow High Street | 41 |
| 'Miriam' – The Sweetheart of Princes Risborough | 47 |

**1944**
| | |
|---|---|
| Wellington at Fox Covert | 51 |
| Dutch Sailors of Gawcott | 53 |
| It's Come Down on Andridge Common (By Julian Evan-Hart) | 56 |
| The Aussie Hero of Quainton | 60 |
| Friendly Fire at Little Chalfont | 65 |
| The Angels of Wing | 68 |

**1945**
| | |
|---|---|
| The Beast of Bourbon | 70 |
| Distinguished Flyers Collide | 73 |
| Double Sacrifice at Taplow | 75 |

**And Still They Fell – Accidents Post WW2**
| | |
|---|---|
| The Sound of a Swallow Over Little Brickhill | 79 |

**Bombs & Rockets**
| | |
|---|---|
| Vengeance Weapons | 84 |

**Appendix I**

| | |
|---|---|
| **Buckinghamshire Incident & Accident Log** | 90 |

| | |
|---|---|
| **Sources & References** | 95 |

# INTRODUCTION

I have been involved in military and aviation research for over 30 years. This publication is the result of a desire to share with the world some of the facts about aircraft accidents and losses in the UK prior to, and throughout, the Second World War. Since the early days of flight Buckinghamshire has witnessed many milestones in aviation history as technological advances were made in the aircraft industries. Names such as Denham and Halton became renowned for their part in the development of many types of air transport over the years, much of which was used for military purposes. The onset of the Second World War saw a massive increase in aircraft development as well as the needs of the Royal Air Force, as pilots and aircrew undertook numerous training, conversion and operational flights. During the early stages of the war the rapid expansion of the aircrew training programme brought with it an unfortunate increase in the number of aviation accidents. Many of these crash sites have been lost to the tide of time and those who witnessed these incidents become fewer with each passing year. As the war progressed a series of new airfields were created from which recently formed units would operate and, as a result, aircraft accidents increased still further. A tour across the county today can, in some cases, bring you face to face with some of these remnants of Britain's air war. Some have been converted to use by light industry and bring prosperity to the towns and villages that once hosted the uniformed hordes of Allied airmen and women. Others have returned to the agricultural land from which they were born. A few have remained exactly as they were left after passing from military use and lay, derelict and decaying, hidden in the fields and woodlands of the counties where they were once so active.

The arrival of the United States Army Air Force in 1942 significantly increased the level of air traffic across the county's airfields as the Americans also carried out training flights and operational missions. Inevitably, this escalating level of flights led to a considerable number of accidents which had both tragic and, in some cases, miraculous outcomes. There are many stories of how battle-weary aircraft, often with wounded men aboard, managed to reach the 'home field' only to suffer traumatic engine failure and crash to earth, just a few hundred yards from safety.

Others were involved in tragic mid-air collisions or incidents where their heavily laden aircraft became uncontrollable shortly after leaving the ground. In these cases there was nearly always significant loss of life, both for those aboard the aircraft as well as those on the ground.

For the civilian population there was also death and danger from the skies, not only due to the fact that they were often in the path of many accidents but that they were also subjected to air raids and attacks brought about by the continuing improvements in enemy weapons technology. I have attempted to cover some of the major incidents that affected the men, women and children of the towns and villages as well as those occasions where their efforts to save the crew of stricken aircraft resulted in an award for bravery. The scope of this book is not intended to be a comprehensive representation of everything that happened concerning aviation history as this would result in a gargantuan tome. I have had to be selective concerning the topics covered, although each incident in itself is unique and reflective of a certain period. There are some areas of minimal detail and where these occur it is most likely due to them having already been covered adequately in other publications, such as particular airfield histories, some subjects may be touched on lightly, whilst others are in themselves highly detailed accounts. Like all books in this series one of the main aims is to ensure that the less publicised events are not lost to history, whilst another is to stimulate interest in subjects that may hopefully lead the reader to conduct personal, detailed research of their own. The author hopes that some of the contents of this volume will be accepted and considered as a very small but important step to prevent the loss of these aspects to our county's aviation history. Concerning research, I would at this stage like to mention that many areas of the text and the crash listings at the end of the volume were produced with reference to official documentation of the period and this, in itself, often contains omissions and errors. I have made every effort, to correct these and ensure that historical accuracy is maintained. It is my hope that I have made some small contribution to retaining Britain's aviation history as well as honouring those who have lost their lives in aircraft accidents in Buckinghamshire.

Paul Johnson

# AIRCRAFT ACCIDENT INVESTIGATION

Captain George Bertram Cockburn OBE

The Accidents Investigation Branch (AIB) was established in 1915 as part of the Royal Flying Corps under the direction of Captain George Bertram Cockburn OBE. He was a research chemist who became an aviation pioneer and represented Great Britain in the first international air race at Rheims in 1909. Unfortunately, Cockburn crashed into a haystack and was unable to complete the course. In 1912 he became a founder member of the Royal Aero Club's Public Safety and Accidents Investigation Committee. He co-founded the first aerodrome for the army at Larkhill and also trained the first four pilots of what was to become the Fleet Air Arm. During World War I he served in France with No.59 Squadron and worked as a Government Inspector of Aeroplanes for the Royal Flying Corps at Farnborough. Cockburn subsequently became head of the Accidents Investigation Branch (AIB) of the Department of the Controller-General of Civil Aviation at the Air Ministry.

At the end of the First World War the Department of Civil Aviation was set up by the Air Ministry and the AIB became part of that department with a remit to investigate both civil and military aviation accidents. Following the Second World War the Ministry of Civil Aviation was established and in 1946 the AIB was transferred to it, but continued to assist the Royal Air Force with accident investigations - a situation which has continued ever since. After working under various parent Ministries the AIB moved to the then Department of Transport in 1983 and in November 1987 its name was changed to the Air Accidents Investigation Branch (AAIB). Latterly, the AAIB has become part of the reorganised Department for Transport (DfT) since 2002.

# THE AIRFIELDS

## Booker

The airfield, originally known as Marlow Airport, was requisitioned by the Air Ministry in 1939 and opened in 1941 as the home of No.21 Elementary Flying Training School. The flying school operated 72 Tiger Moths and Miles Magisters. No.21 EFTS trained 120 pupils on a seven week course. An investigation of the ever increasing number of aircraft accidents identified the fact that training needed to be more comprehensive and later the course was extended to 11 weeks. In May 1942, training was also started on the airfield for the officers and men of the embryo Glider Pilot Regiment who learnt to fly light aircraft before they went on to RAF Croughton for conversion to the all-wood Hotspur gliders. Conversion to the heavier Horsa glider, used during the D-Day landings and the Market Garden operation, took place at RAF Brize Norton. In 1950, the University of London Air Squadron resumed flying out of Booker, and it also temporarily hosted the Manchester and Liverpool University Squadrons. In 1955, a hard runway, made of wide pierced steel planking, was added to the four wartime grass runways. The Bomber Command Communications Flight continued to use Booker until 1963. In 1965 the airfield became privately run and is now Wycombe Air Park.

## Cheddington

The airfield opened on 15th March 1942 as a satellite for No.26 Operational Training Unit at Wing. Both Ansons and Wellingtons were stationed at the airfield until 7th September 1942 when it came under the control of the 8th USAAF. The Ground Echelon of the 44th Bomb Group stayed at Cheddington until October of that year when they moved to Shipdham, Norfolk. The airfield served as home to various of British and American units throughout the early part of 1943 until, on 16th August, it was converted to USAAF Station 113, and became the 8th USAAF Combat Crew Replacement Centre. Between June 1944 and June 1945 a number of specialised American units were based at Cheddington for short periods of time, including the 36th and 406th Bomb Squadrons who flew leaflet dropping and secret operations from the airfield.

Cheddington was finally handed back to the RAF in July 1945. The site was then used for vehicle disposal and accommodation and finally closed in 1952. Today the site is used by light industry although the runways and assorted taxiways, hardstands and aprons have all been removed for hardcore. There are a significant number of wartime buildings in various levels of abandonment on what was the technical site that can be seen on Google Earth, as well as a grass runway that is now used by private light aircraft.

## Denham

Flying has been taking place at this site since the earliest days of aviation. In 1914 the Royal Flying Corps Schools of Aeronautics came to Denham to learn how to pack parachutes and rig aircraft, and in 1915 a flying training school for Flight Cadets was based on the present aerodrome site. At the close of the First World War the land returned to farming, although flying continued, and the site was purchased by Myles Bickerton who built two hangars, installed fuel tanks and built a club house for visiting pilots. Denham became very popular as private owners began to seek storage for their wood and linen aircraft. In 1935 a garden party was held at the aerodrome to celebrate the Silver Jubilee of King George V and Queen Mary. With the threat of war looming aviation activity on the airfield began to increase. The London University Air Squadron, the Volunteer Reserve Flying School and the Civil Air Guard School of Flying all began training flights from Denham in Hawker Harts and Fairey Battles. The Gladiator aerobatic team also flew in occasionally from Hendon to practice. The Martin-Baker Company started aircraft development at Denham and, following the death of Valentine Baker in September 1942, later became the world's most experienced manufacturer of ejection seats and related air safety equipment. Throughout World War II the site expanded as the RAF moved in and five more hangars were built along with a few nissen huts. No.21 Elementary Flying Training School used Denham for its Tiger Moths and many glider pilots were trained there. After the war the aerodrome was abandoned by the Air Ministry and fell into disrepair. It was eventually privately purchased and has operated ever since as a school of flying.

## Halton

In 1913 the owner of the Halton estate, Alfred de Rothschild, invited No.3 Squadron of the Royal Flying Corps to conduct manoeuvres on his land. Following a gentleman's agreement between de Rothschild and Lord Kitchener, the estate was used by the British Army throughout the First World War. By

1916, over 20,000 troops were billeted on the estate under canvas, and later, in wooden huts. Many of these soldiers went on to die during the Somme offensive. Meanwhile, the continuing land battles were demonstrating the value of air power, which resulted in a rapid expansion of the Royal Flying Corps. This created a massive requirement for skilled manpower to keep the ever-increasing number of aircraft entering service in the air. Halton was chosen as the principal training base to meet this demand and was soon pouring out air mechanics in huge numbers – no less than 14,000 in 1917 alone. In the same year, a far sighted decision was taken to establish a boy mechanics' training depot which enlisted boys as young as 15, thus sowing the seeds of Halton's long and distinguished record in training young men in aeronautical engineering trades. The whole estate was purchased by the government for use by the Royal Air Force at the end of the First World War. In 1919 No.1 School of Technical Training was established at RAF Halton and remained there until it moved to RAF Cosford in the early 1990s. At the same time, Halton House was re-opened as the Station's Officers' Mess and continues to be used as the principal Officers' Mess. During World War II RAF Halton continued its training role. Additionally, No.112 Squadron and No.402 Squadron of the Royal Canadian Air Force were based at Halton for part of the war. Halton was also renowned for the Princess Mary Hospital which was opened in 1927. Countless thousands of war casualties were treated at the hospital and, in later years, it treated NHS patients and families of service personnel. The hospital was also renowned as the first specialist burns unit in England, gaining its expertise through treating the injuries of aircrew from World War II. A small laboratory located in Finchley for the study of tropical diseases moved to Halton in 1925 and later became the RAF Pathological Laboratory. In 1935 this unit became the RAF Institute of Pathology & Tropical Medicine. A number of other medical services and training units operated in the hospital until its closure in 1995. Although the buildings still stand, they are derelict and the surrounding married quarters have been sold off for private housing. Today, Halton continues to be one of the most significant bases in the RAF, providing a variety of basic and further training courses for the men and women in its service.

## Little Horwood

The construction of the airfield begun in 1940 and it became fully operational on 3rd September of that year when No.25 Operational Training Unit moved in from RAF Cheddington. The role of the unit was to familiarise aircrew with flying bombers under operational conditions, both by day and night, and for this they used Vickers Wellingtons. Some aircraft from Little Horwood took part in the first 1,000 bomber raids on Germany as well as some other operations. In 1945 the airfield was used by aircraft during Operation Exodus for ferrying British prisoners of war back from Europe. Little Horwood ceased operational duties on 15th January 1946. Today, the site is used for light industrial use and the remnants of the runways and perimeter tracks scar the Buckinghamshire landscape. Plans have been set to develop the area into a housing estate and the airfield will disappear into the annals of aviation history.

### Oakley

Oakley opened on the 27th May 1942, initially as a second satellite to Bicester airfield but in August of that year switched to serve Wescott airfield. No.11 Operational Training Unit were the first occupants of the site and they remained there until the end of the war. During May of 1945 the airfield was used as part of Operation Exodus to ferry Allied PoWs home from the continent and it was here that they first stood on the soil of freedom after their long ordeal. At the close of the operation nearly 17,000 PoWs had landed at the airfield in a variety of Allied aircraft. Oakley closed to flying in August 1945, but remains very visibly a wartime airfield, whose main runway remains largely intact. The airfield also holds one special feature, a well-preserved 'B1' hangar.

### Thame (Haddenham)

CTF Aviation was founded at Haddenham in 1938 and a propeller factory was later built in 1939. In January 1941 the Glider Training Squadron moved to Haddenham from Ringway, later becoming No.1 Glider Training School. In December 1941 the school moved to Croughton. In 1943 the Air Transport Auxiliary pilot training school moved to the airfield from White Waltham and Barton-in-the-Clay, staying until the end of the war. No.5 Ferry Pool of the ATA was also based at Haddenham. In March 1945 the airfield was used by the Overseas Packing Unit and 3rd Reception Centre. Post-war Chartair was founded here in 1946, buying the airfield in 1947 also set up Airtech for aircraft maintenance. Halifaxes and Dakotas were converted for civil use, Airtech remaining here until the 1990s.

### Westcott

RAF Westcott opened in September 1942 and was used by No.11 Operational Training Unit during the Second World War, along with its satellite station RAF Oakley, for the training of bomber crews. Many of the crews who were trained at the airfield later saw active service in Lancaster bombers in the fierce aerial campaign waged by RAF Bomber Command over occupied Europe. The RAF moved out in August 1945 shortly after nearly 53,000 liberated Allied PoWs, who arrived by air, passed through Westcott as the first UK staging post in their repatriation during Operation Exodus. The station closed on 3rd April 1946. In the 1960s and 1970s, it was the home of the Rocket Propulsion Establishment which undertook the design and development of rocket motors, and was responsible for most of the rocket motors used in British guided missiles and research vehicles. In 1984 the Rocket Propulsion Establishment came under the control of the Royal Ordnance Factories, and in 1987 control passed to the private sector when British Aerospace took over Royal Ordnance. The site is now used by light industry.

Wing

RAF Wing opened on 17th November 1941 after the existing airfield was restored. It had two runways and five hangars, although one of these was later destroyed when an aircraft crashed. On 15th January 1942 Wing became home to No.26 Operational Training Unit, part of No.7 Group Bomber Command, when it was formed at the airfield. The first aircraft to use the new runways was a Tiger Moth which landed on 18th March. No.1 Flying Course commenced on 25th April 1942 with a mixture of Ansons and Wellingtons for conversion flying. The airfield also had its own unique aircraft for a few weeks when Captain Valentine Henry Baker, of the Martin-Baker Company, came to Wing in August 1942 to trial the MB3 prototype. Unfortunately, both Baker and the MB3 were lost in a forced landing following engine failure. From September 1942 No.26 OTU started to take part in operational flights from Wing including attacks on Dusseldorf, Bremen and Essen. The unit continued to operate Wellingtons in their various models until the end of the war. The end of the war brought hectic activity to Wing when it was chosen to receive Allied PoWs who were being returned home as part of Operation Exodus. No.26 OTU was eventually disbanded on 4th March 1946 and the airfield began to be wound down. It was used for a while as a bomb dump and there was talk of using the RAF huts for housing, but site was eventually sold in April 1960. In 1963 Stansted had been recommended as the site for London's third airport. This proposal had been ultimately rejected and, in 1969, Wing was included amongst a shortlist of new possible locations. The commission on The Third London Airport led by the High Court Judge, Mr Justice Roskill, had first met in private on 25th June 1968 and shortly after Christmas 1970, Wing became their firm recommendation to the Government for the location of a new airport. There then began an intensive two-year battle by the local communities against the decision. During a meeting, held on the eve of the Roskill announcement, in the drawing room of a local farmer, Bill Manning, the Wing Airport Resistance Association was born. In the following week the WARA officials were inaugurated at a meeting in Winslow and, to publicise the cause, 40,000 pamphlets as well as car stickers were given out. Funds for the campaign were raised from numerous sources including the sale of original Fleet Street cartoons, beetle drives and, at Stewkley, a 'mile of pennies' were laid outside the church, all of which raised a considerable sum. Eventually, after a long and hard struggle, the campaign succeeded and on 26th April 1971 John Davis, the Secretary of State for Trade and Industry, told the House of Commons that the airport would now be built at Foulness Island, Essex. As a permanent celebration of the victory, the Buckinghamshire County Council, following an appeal for contributions, planted a spinney of over 400 trees, on a three acre site that would have been the centre of the airport. Today, this spinney can be clearly seen on Google Earth. The site continues in both agricultural and light industry use, although parts of the old runways and some of the original buildings still remain.

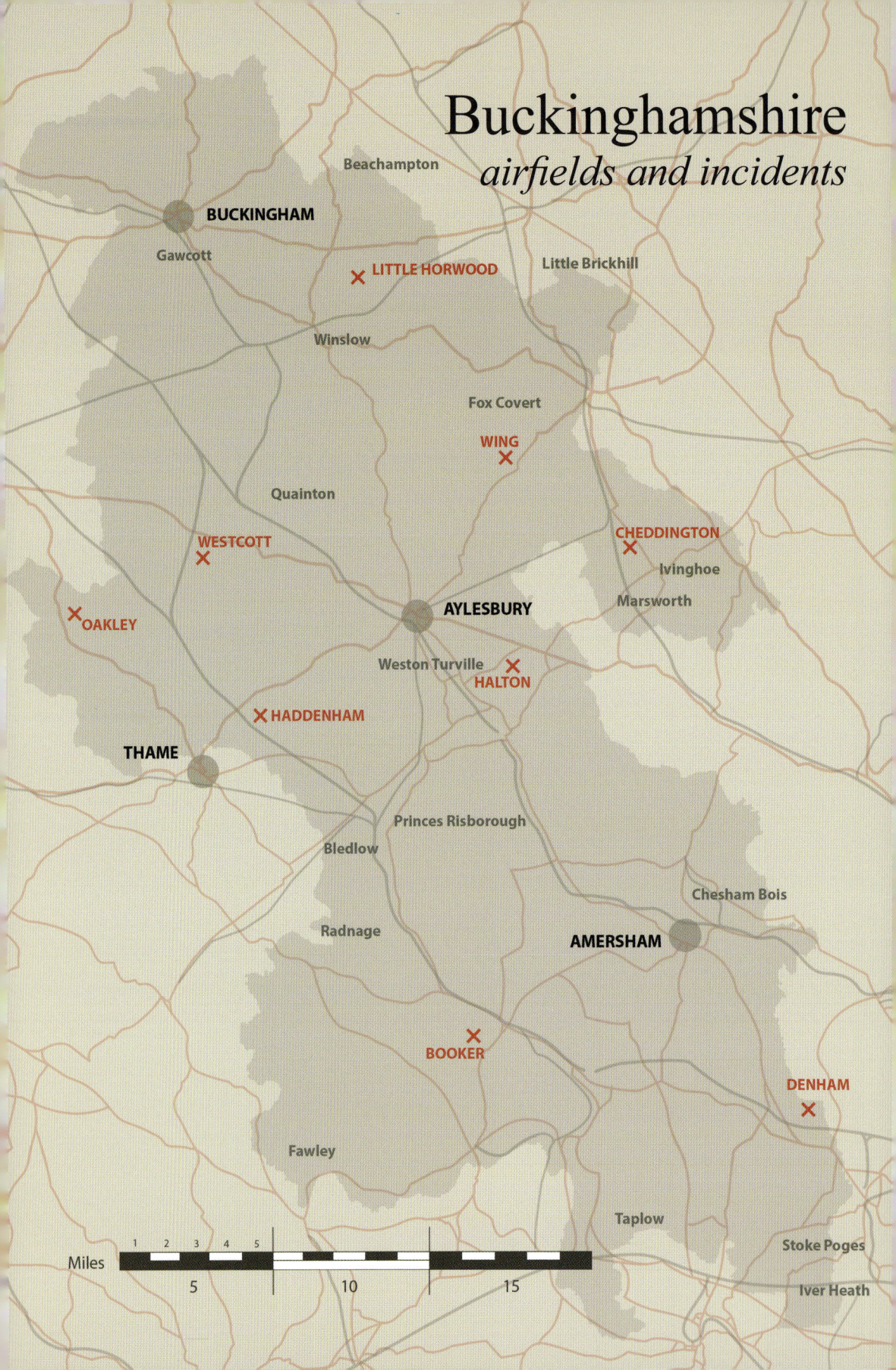

# THE GOLDEN YEARS

## STALL IN A STORM AT IVINGHOE

### 14th September 1923

LOCATION
Ivinghoe

TYPE
De Havilland DH34

SERIAL No.
G-EBBS

UNIT
Daimler Airway

PILOT
Mr. George Edward PRATT
aged 27 - killed

Co-Pilot
Mr. Leslie George Scott ROBINSON
aged 32 - killed

PASSENGERS
Mr. Albert Hayward TURNER
aged 37 - killed
Mr. John GRIMSHAW
aged 37 - killed
Mrs. Ethel Russell ARMITAGE
aged 21 - killed

The Daimler Airway, owned by Daimler Hire Ltd, was the first company to begin operating De Havilland DH.34 single-engined cabin biplanes, in April 1922. A total of six were operated from Croydon Airport London to Paris. From October 1922 until early 1924, the airway operated daily scheduled flights from Alexandra Park Aerodrome, Manchester to Croydon Airport, London. In 1923 Daimler added further routes from Croydon to Amsterdam, Hanover and Berlin using their DH.34 fleet.

The De Havilland DH.34 had a plywood-clad fuselage, a two-man cockpit and was powered by a single Napier Lion engine, which was fitted for inertia starting, avoiding the necessity for hand swinging of the propeller to start the engine. Unusually, the design of the aircraft allowed an entire spare engine to be carried on board across the rear of the passenger cabin. The cabin door's unusual shape was to allow the engine to be loaded and unloaded, and a specially-fitted 'porthole' on the other side of the cabin would be removed to allow the propeller boss to protrude out the side of the aircraft. Spare engines were not carried routinely as the DH.34's payload was too low to carry both passengers and a spare engine, but this facility was used by operators to quickly fly spare engines out to aircraft that had suffered breakdown.

On 14th September 1923 one of these aircraft, G-EBBS, was due to undertake a flight from Croydon to Manchester, carrying three passengers as well as some mail. The crew consisted of the pilot, George Pratt, an experienced flyer who had served in the Royal Air Force between 1918 and 1923 (but who had only been granted his civil pilots license four weeks earlier) and the co-pilot, Leslie Robinson, who had served with the company for a number of years and had many hours of flying experience. After boarding their passengers the crew took off at 17.20 hours for the evening flight to Manchester. The weather conditions at Croydon were described as fair, but just north of London it rapidly deteriorated with low cloud, rain and heavy local storms occurring. George Pratt made his last radio contact with Croydon as he passed over Watford. Witnesses saw the aircraft flying through torrential rain at a very low height between Berkhampstead and Tring, as it followed a course parallel but just north of the railway line.

As the aircraft passed over the village of Ivinghoe the rain ceased, but visibility was still very poor and it was apparent that a heavy storm was approaching from the west. The crew decided to make a landing in a large field on the outskirts of the village and the pilot made a turn to the right in preparation for a decent. As it was making its approach the engine was heard to open up in an effort to avoid some high trees. The aircraft then travelled in a flat glide for about 200 yards towards the field when it suddenly dived into the ground from a height of about 150 feet. The crew and their passengers were killed instantly.

### The Investigation

An accident investigation revealed that, although the crew were very experienced, neither of the pilots had visited the Meteorological Office at Croydon to obtain a weather report before undertaking the flight. This was contrary to normal practice. It was also established that a 400lb ballast bag being carried in the luggage compartment of the aircraft was made up of earth, rubble and concrete. In the investigator's opinion the accident was the result of pilot error when attempting to land the aircraft in bad weather. He also suggested that, in future, the aircraft should carry a standardised form of trimming weight in the tail. The stalling speed of 63 mph was considered high and extensions were fitted to the upper wings of later models. Notwithstanding this, there appeared to be no apparent reason for the crash. Although there was an impending storm, it was not raining when the crash occurred. The aircraft was carrying enough fuel for the flight to Manchester and both George Robinson and George Pratt were experienced pilots who had flown this route on more than one occasion. The aircraft was in good condition, so what had happened?

Above: DH-34 G-EBBS lies in the field at Ford End Farm where it crashed, taking the lives of the crew and passengers. But what caused the accident?

Right: A DH-34 similar to the one that crashed at Ivinghoe.

## The Mysterious Lady

During the coroner's inquest a mystery began to unravel. The Daimler Hire representative, Tristram Beresford, indicated that after the initial crash it was believed that the lady

onboard was the wife of John Grimshaw. It was later established that Grimshaw, a personal secretary for a Mrs Caroline Gudewill, had been separated from his wife for the four months prior to the accident and that she was living in London. Jane Harriett Crook of Norton Terrace, Belgravia, London had identified the body of 21 year-old Ethel Armitage and could not explain why she was onboard the aircraft. Mrs Crook acknowledged that Mrs. Armitage lived with her, because her husband Russell Armitage, had lived in New York for the previous 18 months. John Grimshaw had called at Mrs. Crook's home on several occasions and had 'taken out' Mrs. Armitage. Beresford also established that Mrs. Armitage had recently been in Switzerland and Italy with 'an unknown person'. The coroner attempted to establish what these matters had to do with the accident. Beresford indicated that Mrs. Armitage may have been 'violent' towards Grimshaw in the past and that the pilot had appeared to be attempting a hurried landing. He stated that although there was no evidence as to what had happened inside the little aircraft, perhaps some event amongst the passengers had contributed to the crash.

# 1939

# LYSANDER DISCOVERY AT DENHAM

When the Great War ceased in November 1918 No.13 Squadron remained in France, before returning to the UK in 1919 and disbanding. It was reformed at Kenley in April 1924 and resumed its Army co-operation role with Bristol Fighters, playing a major role in developing co-operation between land and air forces. Atlas, Audaxes and Hectors were subsequently used by the squadron until early 1939 when the new Lysander arrived.

On 28th April 1939, as Britain held its breath at the thought of another European war, Pilot Officer Denys Greville-Bell undertook a trial flight in the new aircraft, with Flight Lieutenant Graham as a passenger. Apart from an unusually steep climb after take-off the flight was uneventful and the aircraft soon returned to the ground. F/Lt Graham then secured the parachute harness and P/O Greville-Bell prepared for a solo flight as part of his conversion training. He taxied out to the main runway at Denham and opened the throttle on the Lysander's single engine. The aircraft left the ground and Greville-Bell again put it into a steep climb. As the aircraft reached a height of about 300 feet the right wing was seen to dip. The nose then swung to the right and the Lysander slammed into the ground before Greville-Bell had a chance to make any correction. He was killed instantly.

### The Discovery

The following morning F/Lt Graham boarded another Lysander and took off from Denham. When at a safe height he set the aircraft's tail trimming gear

---

**28th April 1939**

LOCATION
Denham Airfield

TYPE
Westland Lysander I

SERIAL No.
L4762

UNIT
13 Squadron, Royal Air Force

PILOT
Flying Officer Dennis Greville BELL aged 22 - killed

**Above: The high-wing monoplane Westland Lysander was a major step forward from the old biplanes that 13 Squadron had previously been equipped with.**

to the 'take off' position and placed the propeller to 'fine pitch'. He reduced his speed to about 50mph and then attempted to place the aircraft in a climbing position, similar to that which had taken Greville-Bell's life. As the aircraft's speed reduced, and without warning, the right wing dipped, the Lysander turned 180 degrees and dived very steeply for about 900 feet before he was able to gain control. He attempted this manoeuvre on four separate occasions and each time the aircraft reacted in the same way. F/Lt Graham reported his findings and it is believed that this discovery led to the production of the Mk.II model.

Today, Pilot Officer Greville-Bell lays buried in Odiham Churchyard, Hampshire. As his death occurred prior to 3rd September 1939 he is not officially recorded in the War Dead listings despite the fact that his death may have, inadvertently, led to the saving of many pilots lives.

**Left: Greville-Bell's grave at Odiham Churchyard.**

# 1940

# FORMATION FLYER LOST AT WESTON TURVILLE

On 10th August 1940, as the Battle of Britain raged across the skies of the Home Counties, Squadron Leader Ian Walker was detailed to take part in a Station Defence Exercise, as a pilot of one of five Magisters which were due to represent a bomber formation attacking RAF Halton. His aircraft took off at 11.45hrs and was due to take up the No.2 position at a height of 1000 feet. Evidence was given by Wing Commander Broadbury, the formation leader, that as all the machines were taking up their positions S/Ldr Walker's aircraft was seen to veer to the right then resume its course. The nose of the aircraft then rose up and its left wing dropped. Flight Lieutenant Forester-Walker, who was flying in the No.4 position, stated that the Magister then flipped on to its back and made a vertical dive straight into the ground at Weston Turville. A

Below: The Miles Magister was a two seat basic trainer which was fairly easy to handle, especially for experienced pilots.

## 10th August 1940

**LOCATION**
Weston Turville

**TYPE**
Miles Magister

**SERIAL No.**
N5431

**UNIT**
Headquarters No.24 Group

**PILOT**
Squadron Leader Ian Henry Douglas WALKER   aged 27 - killed

Court of Inquiry could not determine the cause of the accident but felt that 'bumpy' weather conditions had played a part in it.

Squadron Leader Heyman, who was with Walker on the night of 9th August, stated that their night had been very disturbed with a constant flow of telephone calls and air raid warnings. There was some indication that Squadron Leader Walker had been working very hard of late and that fatigue may have contributed to the cause of the accident. However, his wife and those associated with him felt that he was not noticeably tired on 10th August. Air Vice Marshal Paul Maltby, who was commanding No.24 Group at the time, had asked S/Ldr Walker to take the place of another pilot, who had insufficient experience of flying Magister aircraft. There was no evidence of any structural fault with the aircraft and S/Ldr Walker had over 1200 hours of flying experience, including 14 hours on Magisters, so an exact cause for the accident could not be determined. Squadron Leader Walker is buried in Halton Cemetery, Buckinghamshire. Tragically, his brother, Pilot Officer Gavin Walker, was killed on 27th September 1942 whilst flying with No. 1 Photographic Reconnaissance Unit, RAF, and is buried in Tromso Cemetery, Norway.

**Squadron Leader Ian Walker's gravestone at Halton.**

# 1941

# A HURRICANE HITS BLEDLOW THE DEATH OF AN ATA PILOT

As the Second World War began it became obvious to the Air Ministry that they would need pilots to ferry new aircraft to service airfields and military bases across the country, from both manufacturer's airfields and maintenance units. It was not deemed viable to use fully-trained RAF pilots to ferry the aircraft, so the next best option was reluctantly accepted, this was to take on civilians who held a pilot's licence. The Air Transport Auxiliary came into being in September 1939, under the direction of Gerard d' Erlanger, a young banker, private pilot, and director of the British Overseas Airways Corporation.

He had foreseen the possibility of using 'A' rated pilots and commercial pilots who had been stood down, to assist the war effort by carrying mail, important passengers and spare parts. The first recruits included farmers, publicans, journalists and pilots who had served in the Great War, but they were soon in action delivering aircraft from factories and maintenance units to the Fleet Air Arm and the RAF. They began with light aircraft and progressed to cover all twin and four engined machines, flying boats and early jets. Ansons were used mainly to take ATA pilots to collect aircraft and return them afterwards to their bases. The organisation grew speedily and in January 1940 eight women were recruited, soon to be joined by others, including Amy

| 17th March 1941 |
|---|
| LOCATION |
| Holly Green, Bledlow |
| TYPE |
| Hawker Hurricane I |
| SERIAL No. |
| Z7010 |
| UNIT |
| Ex.Custody RAF Henlow |
| PILOT |
| First Officer Percy RANDALL (ATA) aged 40 - killed |

Right: Percy Randall.

Johnson who met her death in the Thames Estuary in 1941 while ferrying an Oxford.

According to official records it was thought that it would take 624 civilians to replace twelve RAF pilots. For this target to be reached, it was finally agreed that the civilian pilots had to be recruited, rather than called up, to ensure the quality of the flying skills of the applicants and allow a rank structure to be based on experience. An ATA ferry pool was soon set up at White Waltham, west of London. From here they could service the aircraft factories in the Midlands and southern England. White Waltham was to become No.1 Ferry Pool as well as the administrative headquarters and the conversion school for the ATA.

Amongst the first recruits to this new service was Percy Randall who was born on 26th May 1900 in Englefield Green, Surrey. By 1933 he was the owner of a garage in Southsea, Hampshire and had joined the Portsmouth Aero Club, which had been formed in October 1931. On 28th August 1933 Percy was granted his Pilot's Certificate, which was numbered 11354, obtained whilst using a de Havilland DH60 'Gipsy Moth'. Percy went on to perform numerous ferry flights during his time with the ATA.

On 16th March 1941 Percy Randall undertook a ferry flight in a Hurricane from RAF Henlow to White Waltham. The following extract is from the report made by the Accidents Investigation Branch after their visit to the crash site, two days after it occurred;

*"The facts which have been determined by the investigation, or which the available evidence is considered to establish, are as follows:- The log books were in the aeroplane and were lost in the accident. Form 700 and the remnants of papers salvaged showed that the airframe was Canadian built, had flown 1hr. 25 min. and that the engine had run 138 hrs. The pilot was a civilian, 40 years of age, employed by the Air Transport Auxiliary. According to his history record card he had a total flying time of 551 hrs, 22 hrs. of which had been in Hurricanes. He had flown 26 different types of aircraft, held an "A" licence and was considered reliable and exceptionally capable. At the time of the accident weather*

conditions in the locality were bad for flying. The 1300 hr. report from Benson was "Slight haze, visibility 2000 - 4000 yards, clouds 10/10ths at 500 feet", and from Bicester "Rain and fog, visibility 500 - 1000 yards, sky obscured". The wind was E.N.E. about 5 m.p.h. On the evening before the accident the pilot collected the aircraft from Henlow for delivery to White Waltham. Here the sound of his engine was heard overhead but fog prevented a landing and he went away. He later rang up to say he had landed at Luton and he spent the night there. Between 1000 and 1030 hrs on the following morning the pilot was in communication by telephone with the Officer Commanding No, 1 F.P.P. He was told that the weather at White Waltham was bad and that he should stand by at Luton and bring his aircraft away if the weather cleared.

He was further told that if there was no improvement a car would be sent for him later that day as, although there was no particular urgency about the delivery of the aircraft, he was wanted back for other reasons.

About midday the pilot made a telephone call from the duty pilot's office at Luton. It is not known to whom he spoke but he told the duty officer that the weather was all right at White Waltham and that he proposed to start. He stated that if after all he could not get through to White Waltham he might land at Hullavington. At this time the conditions for flying at Luton were improving but were still bad and had it not been that he carried an authority allowing him to authorise his own flight it is unlikely the pilot would have been permitted to leave. (All A.T.A. pilots, except novices, carry a permit authorising them to decide whether or not they will leave the aerodrome.)

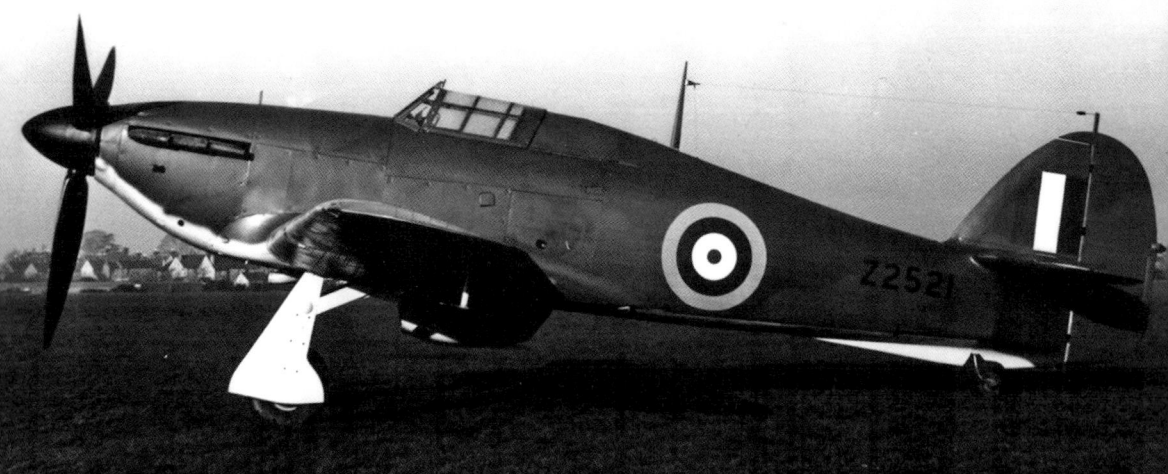

Below: A factory fresh Z serialled Hurricane similar to the one in which Percy Randall lost his life.

Right: Percy Randall's Pilot's Certificate.

```
RANDALL, Percy.                                      11354

    Plaza Garage, Britannia Road, Southsea.


Born      26th May, 1900.      at    Englefield Green.
Nationality      British.
Rank, Regiment, Profession    Garage Proprietor.
Certificate taken on      D·H·60.Gipsy.11. 105.H.P.
At   Portsmouth Aero Club.
Date   28.8.1933.
```

*He left the ground at about 1315 hrs and shortly afterwards his aircraft came out of clouds and from over the hills by Princes Risborough. He circled over the lower ground for seven minutes under the clouds, the base of which was about 200 feet. The sound of the engine then ceased and the aircraft dived into the ground.*

*Examination at the scene of the accident showed that the aircraft had struck the ground at a steep angle and at high speed. The planes and fuselage were telescoped and the engine was buried deeply in soft clay. Examination of the wreckage was difficult, nevertheless nothing was found to suggest the failure in the air of the airframe or its controls. As the engine had been running almost up to the moment of impact and as its recovery was so difficult it was not considered necessary to extricate it. The pilot had been thrown 15 yards ahead of the crash; his parachute had broken away and was lying by his side unopened. His map was found about 800 yards and his peaked Service cap about 280 yards from the scene of the accident. This is suggestive that he had opened the cockpit hood in flight and that his cap had blown off and that he lost his map at the same time. Note: This is not the first time the pilot of a Hurricane has lost his map in this way. Opinion. The accident was due to the aircraft striking the ground in an incipient spin after the pilot had stalled it in conditions of bad visibility."*

Percy Randall's grave can be found in Maidenhead Cemetery, Berkshire, along with a number of other ATA pilots.

# 1942

# A SUMMER OF GALLANT CIVILIANS

Amongst the many thousands of records held in the British National Archives are a series of recommendations for gallantry awards to civilians for their part in the rescuing crews of aircraft involved in accidents. Several of these incidents occurred in Buckinghamshire during the summer of 1942, a time when the country had its back to the wall. The war was going badly for Britain and Winston Churchill was fearful that morale was being sapped across the country. Each incident resulted in an entry in the London Gazette with a variety of awards being made to the rescuers. Curiously, at least one of these brave men received no recorded recognition for his part in the incident.

On the morning of 3rd July 1942 James Pithers, a 45 year-old farm worker from Amerdon Ponds, Taplow was working in a field on the south side of the Bath Road, about 200 yards away from the railway bridge, when he heard the roaring sound of an aircraft engine. As he looked up he could see a small yellow plane flying at a very low level, directly towards him. The aircraft just cleared the railway tracks, narrowly missing a train that was travelling westwards. It then struck the railway telegraph wires, burst into flames, somersaulted completely and hit a fence on the north side of the Bath Road, whereupon it smashed onto the main carriageway. At the same time 28 year-old Sergeant Sidney Cornelius of the Pioneer Corps was travelling along the Bath Road on his motor cycle, towards Maidenhead. Cornelius later stated that he could see the pilot's upper body as far as his waist, suggesting that he was standing up in his cockpit, possibly in an effort to jump from the stricken plane. Cornelius and Pithers ran to the scene of the accident where they found the pilot trapped under the blazing aircraft. The heat was intense and, initially, they could not reach the trapped flyer but, suddenly, the wind changed and the two men were able to move some wreckage and grab the lifeless body.

**Opposite page: The Miles Magister had open cockpits so it was easy to see the pilot, especially if he was standing on his seat as reports seem to suggest.**

[ 26 ]   WAR TORN SKIES OF GREAT BRITAIN

## 3rd July 1942

**LOCATION**
Taplow

**TYPE**
Miles Magister

**SERIAL No.**
R1889

**UNIT**
21 Elementary Flying Training School

**PILOT**
Sergeant Alexander Galbraith TERRY - 1st Glider Pilot Regiment aged 20 - killed

**ON THE GROUND**
Rescuer: Mr James Damon PITHERS aged 45
Rescuer: Sergeant Sidney George CORNELIUS aged 28

By this time they had been joined by three other men, Percy Dance, Harry Wyse and a Private Lawrence who aided in the rescue. Together, the men managed to haul the body from the inferno but it was too late, Sergeant Terry had suffered considerable head injuries and probably died when the aircraft first struck the ground. His body is buried in the Kilkerran Cemetery, Campbeltown, Argyllshire.

The official entry in the London Gazette of 4th January 1943 reads as follows;

*"Commendations. Those named below have been Commended for brave conduct when attempting to rescue the crews of crashed and burning aircraft: — James Daymen Pithers, Farm Labourer, Taplow, Bucks."*

There is no explanation as to why James Pithers was the only one of the rescuers to receive a commendation, but should you ever pass under the railway bridge at Taplow, spare a thought for all of those who tried to save the life of Alexander Terry all those summers ago.

On the afternoon of 30th August 1942 a twin-engined Wellington bomber of No.26 Operational Training Unit took to the air for a short circuit and landing training flight. Aboard the aircraft was Canadian pilot, Sgt Ron McDougall, and his navigator, Sgt Arnold Hendriksen. At the same time as the aircraft took off a local farmer, William Miller, and his cowman, Daniel Millins, were working in the cowshed at Manor Farm, Marsworth, a small village located at the very edge of Cheddington airfield. The two men were accustomed to the sound of low flying aircraft, so it was not unusual to hear a Wellington making a low approach to the airfield. However, this day was to bring drama, heroism and tragedy to the small community. As Sgt McDougall brought the aircraft in to land it touched down and then bounced slightly back into the air. Realising that the aircraft was in danger, the pilot pushed his throttles forward with the intention of going around again, but just after clearing a hedge he allowed his airspeed to drop and the Wellington stalled and smashed into the ground, just 150 yards from Manor Farm. The aircraft immediately burst into flames, trapping both the pilot, who had been stunned by the force of the impact, and the navigator who had suffered a broken leg and whose clothing was set alight by blazing fuel. Bill Miller and Dan Millins ran across the field to the stricken aircraft and climbed onto the cockpit cover. As they did so, they managed to spot a man struggling inside the burning plane.

At this precise moment an exploding fuel tank blew both men to the ground, delaying their efforts. Undeterred, the two men again climbed up onto the aircraft and Bill Miller reached into the cockpit, where he grabbed the hand of Sgt McDougall and, with the help of Millins, pulled the young Canadian, who was shouting 'Get him out', from the burning wreckage and carried him to safety. Although small arms ammunition was exploding all around them they

## 30th August 1942

**LOCATION**
Manor Farm, Marsworth

**TYPE**
Vickers Wellington Ic

**SERIAL No.**
DV825

**UNIT**
26 Operational Training Unit

**PILOT**
Sergeant Ronald Victor McDOUGALL RCAF aged 22 - injured

**CREW**
Sergeant Arnold Peter HENDRIKSEN aged 20 - died of injuries

**ON THE GROUND**
Rescuer: Mr William Gordon MILLER BEM aged 23

Rescuer: Mr Daniel Ernest MILLINS BEM aged 28

**Above: By August 1942, the Vickers Wellington MkI was the the most common bomber type flying with the OTUs.**

quickly returned to the aircraft where they could hear a man groaning. Due to the fumes and the intensity of the fire they were unable to reach Sgt Hendriksen at first. Eventually, after several attempts, the navigator, whose clothing was now fully on fire, managed to crawl through a hole where a wing had been torn from the fuselage. As he did so the two rescuers dashed forward and grabbed him. Dan Millins then put the fire out with his bare hands but the young navigator was very severely burned. Sgt Hendriksen was taken to the Princess Mary's Hospital, Halton where he died from his injuries on 5th September 1942. He is buried in the St. John The Baptist Churchyard, Malden, Surrey. Sgt McDougall went on to receive a commission and later served with 166 Squadron. Tragically, he was killed in action on 23rd April 1944 during an operation to Dusseldorf and is buried in the Heverlee Cemetery, Belgium.

The official entry in the London Gazette of the 4th January 1943 reads as follows;

*Awarded the British Empire Medal (Civil Division):—*

*William Gordon Miller, Farmer, Marsworth, Buckinghamshire.*

*Daniel Ernest Millins, Farm Labourer, Marsworth, Buckinghamshire.*

*An aircraft crashed in a field and immediately caught fire. Miller and Millins, who were nearby, ran to the burning machine and climbed on to the cockpit cover. They were blown off by an explosion but climbed up again and Miller, leaning through the hatch, caught hold of a man. With Millins' help, he pulled him out and carried him to safety. They then returned to the aircraft and, with great difficulty, extricated another man whose clothing was on fire. Millins extinguished the flames with his hands. Miller and Millins showed courage and determination in the face of fire and exploding petrol-tanks and ammunition.*

William Miller died in 1949 aged just 41 whilst Dan Millins passed away at the age of 60 in 1974.

On Friday 18th September 1942 2nd Lt John Jones was piloting a Tiger Moth (T6821) in company with another similar aircraft. When the two aircraft were in the vicinity of Aylesbury, and flying at a height of about 2,000 feet, the Tiger Moth suddenly went into a steep dive. Try as he might, 2/Lt Jones was unable to recover from the dive and soon realised that the aircraft was going to crash. It was too late for him to bale out, so he did all he could to prepare for the inevitable. As the small plane hurtled towards the ground he switched off the fuel supply, cut the engine and placed his forearm over his face, hoping that he may survive the accident.

On the ground three local men, Henry Read, George Kent and Frank Alcock, looked on in horror as they witnessed the Tiger Moth in distress. They were working in the grounds of Hartwell Park when the aircraft nose-dived into the ground about 100 yards from Hartwell House, where the wreckage burst into flames. 2/Lt Jones had survived the impact but had suffered a fractured leg, as well as other superficial injuries, and was unable to extract himself from the crushed cockpit and was in serious danger of being burned to death. The three men ran to the crash site, where they saw the wreckage ablaze. Alcock and Read jumped onto the wings and grabbed the pilot by his harness straps and hauled him out. George Kent then grabbed the pilot's legs and the three men carried him a short distance in order that he could be given first aid. As they lay him on the ground the aircraft's fuel tank exploded in a ball of flame and the remaining wreckage was totally burned out. Following his fortunate rescue 2/Lt Jones was taken to Stoke Mandeville Hospital where he was treated for his injuries.

The official entry in the London Gazette of the 15th January 1943 reads as follows;

---

**18th September 1942**

LOCATION
Hartwell House, Aylesbury

TYPE
de Havilland Tiger Moth

SERIAL No.
T6821

UNIT
1 Elementary Flying Training School

PILOT
2nd Lieutenant John Gould Whitfield JONES (Army Co-Operation - 19th Field Regiment. Royal Artillery)

ON THE GROUND
Rescuer: Mr Frank ALCOCK aged 44
Rescuer: Mr Henry READ
Rescuer: Mr George KENT

*"Commendations. Those named below have been Commended for brave conduct when attempting to rescue the crews of crashed and burning aircraft: — Frank Alcock, Bricklayer, Aylesbury, Bucks, George Sidney Kent, Bricklayer, Aylesbury, Bucks, Henry William George Read, General Foreman, Aylesbury, Bucks."*

Frank Alcock lived a long and full life eventually passing away in July 1987 at the age of 99.

Below: The Tiger Moth was the first aircraft flown by many of the RAF's pilots during the Second World War, equipping most of the Elementary Flying Training Schools across the country.

# "MY DEAR VAL" - THE DEATH OF VALENTINE HENRY BAKER

## The Aircraft

The Martin-Baker MB3 was a British fighter project with the serial number R2492, and was temporarily stationed at No.26 Operational Training Unit, RAF Wing for trials. It first flew from the station on August 31st 1942. Using lessons learned from the previous MB1 and MB2 models, James Martin and Captain Valentine Baker capitalised on the model and construction to develop the new design, which was powered by a 2,000 Horse Power, Napier Sabre 24-cylinder, H-type engine, driving a de Havilland three-blade propeller. It was armed with six 20-mm cannon mounted in the wings, each with 200 rounds of ammunition, which made it the most heavily armed fighter in existence at the time.

> **18th September 1942**
>
> LOCATION
> Wing
> TYPE
> Martin-Baker M.B.3 Prototype
> SERIAL No.
> R2492
> PILOT
> Valentine Henry BAKER aged 54 - killed

## The Pilot

Valentine Henry Baker was born at Llanfairfechan in North Wales on 24th August 1888, the son of John and Jane Baker. When the Great War broke out, he enlisted in the Royal Navy where he served as a dispatch rider, eventually being promoted to the rank of petty officer. In 1915, in the fighting on the beaches of Gallipoli, he was severely wounded by a bullet in the neck. The doctors considered that any operation to remove the bullet would be fatal, as it had lodged near the spinal cord. Baker told them to 'leave it alone', and the bullet remained in the back of his neck until the day he died. Following this injury he was discharged as unfit, but was soon accepted by the 12th Battalion Royal Welsh Fusiliers, becoming a second lieutenant before the year was out. In 1916, an opportunity came for an entry into aviation and he was posted to the School of Aero Flying at Reading for flying training. On 25th September, 1916, Baker graduated

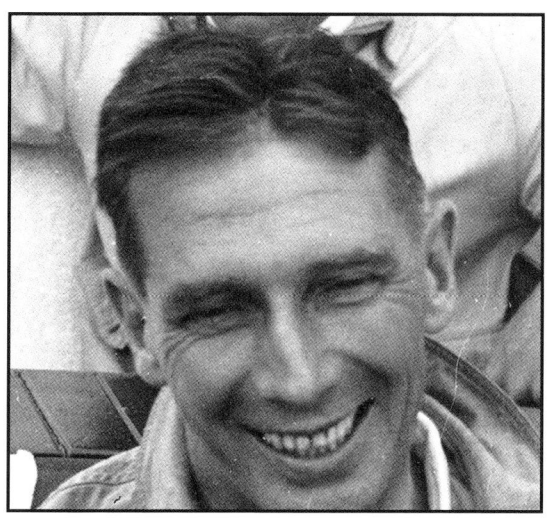

Above: Valentine Henry Baker.

as a flying officer in the Royal Flying Corps. A month later he joined the famous No.41 Squadron at Gosport, with which he was to do all his operational flying and win his Military Cross and later the Air Force Cross.

His first civilian flying job, as a representative of the Vickers-Armstrongs Aircraft Company, took him out to the Dutch East Indies, where he subsequently became attached to the Dutch Naval and Military Air Forces in Java as a flying instructor. After three years, he returned to England, but was soon off again, this time to Chile, where once more he combined demonstrations of new Vickers aircraft with flying instruction. On return to England, Baker became a flying instructor at the Lancashire Flying Club, which he helped to build up, then chief instructor at the London Aeroplane Club at Stag Lane Aerodrome, Edgware. Baker's last, and most important, teaching job came in 1929, when he opened a school and became chief pilot and instructor for Airwork Limited, at Heston Aerodrome. Valentine Baker gave up his instruction flying in 1934 to join his friend James Martin in the formation of a new company, the Martin-Baker Aircraft Company Ltd. The incomparable flying experience and skill possessed by Baker was of great importance in the development and flight testing of the company's prototypes. Over the next eight years, a deep and lasting friendship was to develop between these two men, who were in some ways very similar, in others very different, but each with a great respect for the other's considerable skill and ability.

### The Accident

On Saturday 12th September 1942, Captain Valentine Baker, took the aircraft on a high speed trial flight from RAF Wing, at an altitude of 2,000 feet. After 38 minutes in the air he returned to the airfield where he allowed the engine to 'tick over' whilst some minor adjustments were made. He was then asked to run the engine to full revs the next time he started it, in order to clear any oil residue through the exhausts. At 17.35 hours he re-started the engine and ran it up to 3,000 rpm. He then waved 'chocks away' before running the engine up to full power and having his windscreen wiped, which was the usual practice after clearing surplus oil. Baker took off from Wing to give the aircraft its ninth trial flight, this time being a high speed level trial at 20,000 feet. Although the take off was a little slower than usual, there was no indication that there was anything wrong with the engine or aircraft.

Just after leaving the ground the undercarriage locked up into the wings but the engine immediately started to emit white smoke and began to falter. Baker managed to hold a straight course and reached a height of about 150 feet, where he turned the stricken aircraft to port in an effort to make a landing in a nearby field. As he did so the engine cut out completely. The port wing tip then struck the ground. This was at a point where the aircraft was just 30ft short of a hedge bordering a field in which Baker could have made a successful 'wheels up' landing. The port wing then struck a haystack and the aircraft slewed around and hurtled through the hedge where it turned over and the engine and tail unit broke off. The fuselage then burst into flames, killing the pilot.

### Eye Witnesses

Ground-crewman George Bignall recalled, "Although nobody was allowed into the aircraft hangar, we were able to see it during its testing time. It was very fast with Captain Baker flying very close at times, shooting up the runway very low." On the day of the accident he said, "I was doing a modification on dispersals when Captain Baker took off towards Stewkley. I watched him climb then suddenly the engine cut out and he crashed, trying to land."

Civilian John Thornton also witnessed the accident; "Two fields from where Morris and I were harvesting there was a stack of newly-threshed straw. The MB3 hit this and burst into flame. 'Bunny' Winter, the bailiff of Cold Harbour Farm, beat us to the crash, but we were too late to rescue Captain Baker in the fierce fire."

The onlookers dropped everything and jumped onto their motorbikes or just ran. When they reached the tree line it was all over. The top of the cabin was embedded in a bank and the fuselage, with about 120 gallons of high octane fuel, was ablaze. James Martin, on seeing what had happened, flung himself onto a grass bank and lay there sobbing. 'My dear Val, my dear Val,' over and over again. When the heat died down the rescuers were

**Below: The sleek lines of the MB3 are very apparent in this view.**

able to venture forward to the wreckage. It soon became clear that Baker must have been killed or knocked unconscious instantly and had not had to suffer the agony of burning to death as they had feared. His shoulder harness had been attached to the aircraft fuselage behind him, and it had ripped through the panelling like a knife and was hanging loose. Baker would have been thrown forward, and would have smashed his head as he hit the front of the cockpit. They got stakes of wood out of a nearby fence to try and prise his body out. His shrivelled and charred remains rolled down the wing stub and hit the ground. His body had been burned to less than half its size. Many of the men had seen crashes before, but nothing like this. It was utterly gruesome and horrific and they all felt sick and distressed. Eventually they returned to the hangar as nobody knew quite what to do next. James Martin was there, a solitary figure, walking up and down, apparently oblivious to what was going on as Baker's death had an incalculable effect on him. The horror of the crash, the heat of the blazing aircraft, the stench of burning flesh, were enough to make an indelible impression on those who only knew Baker as James's partner and his dearest friend. More than this, his dear Baker had been killed flying an aeroplane that Martin had designed and built with his own hands. It was of course, the failure of the Napier engine that had caused the crash, not any defect in the aircraft itself, but it still remained that he had died flying one of James's aeroplanes. The subsequent Court of Inquiry found the cause of the crash to be engine failure due to a broken sleeve drive crank in the engine.

## The Outcome

The fatal crash of the prototype was to have a longstanding positive effect on military aviation for decades. After the accident James Martin, who deeply felt the loss of his best friend and partner, developed a passionate interest in the safety of aircrews and he devoted the remainder of his life to the invention and development of the successful Martin-Baker ejection seats. Since the first live ejection test in 1946, a total of 7,334 lives have been saved by Martin-Baker ejection seats. A record that I am sure Val Baker would have been proud of.

*I am indebted to the Martin-Baker Company for their support and co-operation in producing this chapter.*
*Source: Martin-Baker Co.*

# 1943

# GEORGE MEDAL WON AT FAWLEY

**Above: Flying Officer Geoffrey Osborn**

During the Second World War RAF Tempsford was home to No.138 and No.161 'Special Duties' Squadrons. It was from here that SOE (Special Operations Executive) agents and their supplies were flown, and dropped into enemy occupied Europe. Tempsford Airfield has long since been returned to private agricultural use, so passers-by today can be excused for not knowing just what activities went on there between 1941 and 1945. Over eighty aircraft were lost from Tempsford during the war, with many of their crews being killed. Some of these losses were as a result of accidents during both operational and non-operational flights.

One notable accident was on the night of 15th March 1943 when a Handley-Page Halifax took off from Tempsford on an SOE supply drop operation over France, codenamed Director 34. After being in the air for half an hour the aircraft began to suffer engine trouble and the pilot, F/O Geoffrey Osborn, ordered the load of containers to be jettisoned. This action, however, did little to help the situation, the engine failed completely and the aircraft could not maintain height. F/O Osborn struggled to keep the huge bomber in the air and eventually was forced to bring it down at Fawley, Buckinghamshire, three miles north-west of Henley-on-Thames. Sadly, the wireless operator, Sgt Hugh Shearer and the air gunner Sgt Barrie Crane were both killed in the crash landing. The wreckage then caught fire and most of the injured were pulled clear by F/O Osborn.

The pilot was recommended for a gallantry award, but he received the George Medal, the details of which were published in the London Gazette on 13th July 1943. The citation reads as follows;

*Buckinghamshire*

*"This officer has on two occasions displayed great gallantry in rescuing members of his crew from burning aircraft. When serving as an instructor at an Operational Training Unit, he was engaged in testing a Whitley, which crashed and burst into flames. Flying Officer Osborn, who was thrown clear and was uninjured, immediately reentered the aircraft and dragged clear the observer, who was badly injured. In effecting this rescue, Flying Officer Osborn suffered severe burns about the hands and was in hospital for six weeks. In March, 1943, Flying Officer Osborn was captain and pilot of an aircraft which crashed shortly after taking off on an operational flight. The aircraft was soon enveloped in flames and ammunition and Verey lights were exploding, Flying Officer Osborn was dazed but succeeded in extricating four injured members of the crew from the wreckage. In so doing he was badly burnt about the hands, arms and face. Though in a state bordering on collapse, he did all he could to ensure that every member of his crew had been extricated before he was finally persuaded to receive attention."*

Sgt Crane is buried in the Brookwood Military Cemetery, Surrey and Sgt Shearer is buried in his home town of Falmouth, Cornwall.

### Geoffrey Osborn - A Life After the Crash

Geoffrey Alan Osborn was born on January 24th, 1922. His family left for Bermuda when he was seven and he was educated there at Warwick Academy. In 1938 he joined the Bermuda Volunteer Regiment and was mobilised in August the next year. He was a member of a pioneering group of airmen who learned to fly at the Bermuda Flying School at Darrell's Island, leaving for England in 1940. Osborn joined No. 51 Squadron, equipped with the Whitley bomber, and attacked targets in Germany and capital ships operating from the French Biscay ports. On the night of February 27th 1942 he was the second pilot of a Whitley on Operation 'Biting', which dropped paratroops on the German radar site at Bruneval in northern France. Key components of the radar were recovered during this daring raid. After joining No. 161 he flew a number of long-range sorties to drop supplies and agents to the Resistance in France and Belgium. He also dropped supplies to Czech resistors at Pilsen.

---

## 15th March 1943

**LOCATION**
Fawley

**TYPE**
Handley-Page Halifax Mk V

**SERIAL No.**
DG283 MA-Y

**PILOT**
Flying Officer Geoffrey Alan OSBORN GM
Injured, severe burns

**CREW**
Sergeant Barrie Lincoln CRANE (Air Gunner) aged 21 - killed
Sergeant R. POLTOCK (Air Bomber) - Injured, Concussion
Sergeant Hugh SHEARER (Wireless Operator) aged 20 - killed
Flight Sergeant STEVENS (Flight Engineer) - Injured, Concussion
Flying Officer D. THORNTON (Navigator) - Injured, Fractured Femur

---

[ 38 ]   WAR TORN SKIES OF GREAT BRITAIN

Following his crash, he spent many weeks in hospital recovering from his injuries and did not return to operational flying. During his hospital treatment he met Beatrice 'Bobbi' Durham, a member of the nursing staff, and they married in 1944. He was transferred to training duties before returning to Bermuda to operate transport aircraft. He was released from the RAF in May 1946. After the war he initially worked at Kindley Field with Pan American before returning to Britain to become an air traffic controller. He worked in Germany and in Northern Rhodesia before taking up a training role at Stansted and Heathrow Airports. Osborn returned to Bermuda in 1966 to join the Department of Civil Aviation at Kindley Field Airport, becoming Director of Civil Aviation and subsequently Permanent Secretary for Transport. He retired to Dorset in 1985. Geoffrey Osborn was also an internationally noted stamp collector. He amassed a magnificent collection for Gibraltar, which was exhibited in London in 1980. After this was sold he concentrated on creating a superb collection of Bermuda stamps. He was also deeply interested in postal history, contributing to Morris Ludington's book The Postal History and Stamps of Bermuda, and co-authoring the 1971 book The Royal Mail Steam Packets to Bermuda & Bahamas. He also wrote Gibraltar: The Postal History and Naval Officers' Letters: A Study of Letters Sent to and from British Royal Navy Officers Serving Abroad in the Victorian Era. Geoffrey Osborn died on June 16th 2011.

Below: A Special Duties Halifax V similar to the one that crashed at Fawley.

# FOGGY NIGHT AT MURSLEY WATER TOWER

The Mursley water tower was built by the Buckinghamshire Water Board in 1938. In 1940 the Air Ministry authorised the building of Little Horwood airfield, which became operational on 3rd September of that year. The water tower was used by many trainee pilots as a landmark, particularly at night. On 11th April, 1943 a Wellington Mk.III bomber, BJ879, took off from Little Horwood to carry out night dual circuits and landings. At the controls was an experienced pilot, P/O Dennis Bint, who had won the Distinguished Flying Medal in August 1942 whilst serving with No.150 Squadron. The conditions were very foggy and the Wellington twice attempted to land, each time making a dangerous and low approach to the airfield. On the third attempt it was given permission to land and the pilot made a similar approach but suddenly there was a blinding flash in the sky followed by an explosion as the Wellington smashed into the water tower and crashed to the ground, eventually coming to rest 500 yards from the station threshold. All the crew perished in the accident. The crash blackened the exterior of the tower and distorted some of the large pipes and, although repairs were swiftly made and the tower was back working within a week, it was not until a renovation of the tower in 1968 that the wartime scars were finally removed.

In 1995 Anglian Water, who owns the tower, decided to open it to the public for half a day and also set about providing a memorial plaque to honour those that perished in the accident. Relatives of the aircrew were contacted and 1,000 local people attended the memorial service, during which a plaque to the crew was uncovered.

### 11th April 1943

**LOCATION**
Mursley Water Tower, Little Horwood

**TYPE**
Vickers Wellington III

**SERIAL No.**
BJ879

**UNIT**
26 Operational Training Unit

**PILOT**
Pilot Officer Dennis Edward John BINT DFM   aged 20 - killed

**CREW**
Sergeant Francis Bernard McHUGH aged 21 - killed
Sergeant Cyril John FOX aged 22 - killed
Sergeant Joseph Leonin Lionel BELANGER RCAF aged 23 - killed

# BLAZING WIMPEY IN WINSLOW HIGH STREET

## 7th August 1943

**LOCATION**
Winslow

**TYPE**
Wellington III

**SERIAL No.**
X3790

**UNIT**
26 Operational Training Unit

**PILOT**
Sergeant Wilfred DAVIES
aged 22 - killed

**CREW**
Sergeant Jeffery HARRINGTON aged 18 - survived
Sergeant John York SOWTER aged 19 - killed
Sergeant John Patrick Valentine McKEON aged 31 - killed
Sergeant Clive Henry Charles FIETZ RAAF aged 24 - killed

Since the early days of September 1940 the residents of Winslow had grown accustomed to the sights and sounds of Wellington bombers as they flew in and out of the nearby airfields of Little Horwood and Wing. The pilots and crews, nearing the end of their training, would fly both day and night exercises as well as operational missions into enemy territory, so it was not unusual to hear damaged aircraft limping back to their bases. It was on a warm Saturday night in the summer of 1943 that a training exercise was to bring tragedy and devastation to the small historic town.

On 7th August 1943 Wellington X3790 took off from Little Horwood airfield on a routine night flying exercise. The captain of the five man crew was 22 year-old Sgt Wilfred Davies.

Sgt McKeon had recently joined the crew as a replacement for Sgt Samuel Smith, killed on 30 July 1943 when he walked into the arc of a still revolving propeller.

At 02.55 hours the Wellington was returning to the airfield and made its approach but overshot the runway. The pilot then lost control of the aircraft and a few moments later it struck a tree. It smashed into the High Street of Winslow where it totally demolished the Chandos Arms Public House, crashed through a row of cottages that stood back from the road and came to a shuddering halt in a potato field. The townspeople, awakened by the crash, were quickly on the scene but fierce fires had instantly broken out and it was impossible to enter the blazing buildings. The National Fire Service was called, and the local pump was soon on the scene. Other pumps soon arrived

*Buckinghamshire*

A Wellington bomber similar to the one that crashed at Winslow.

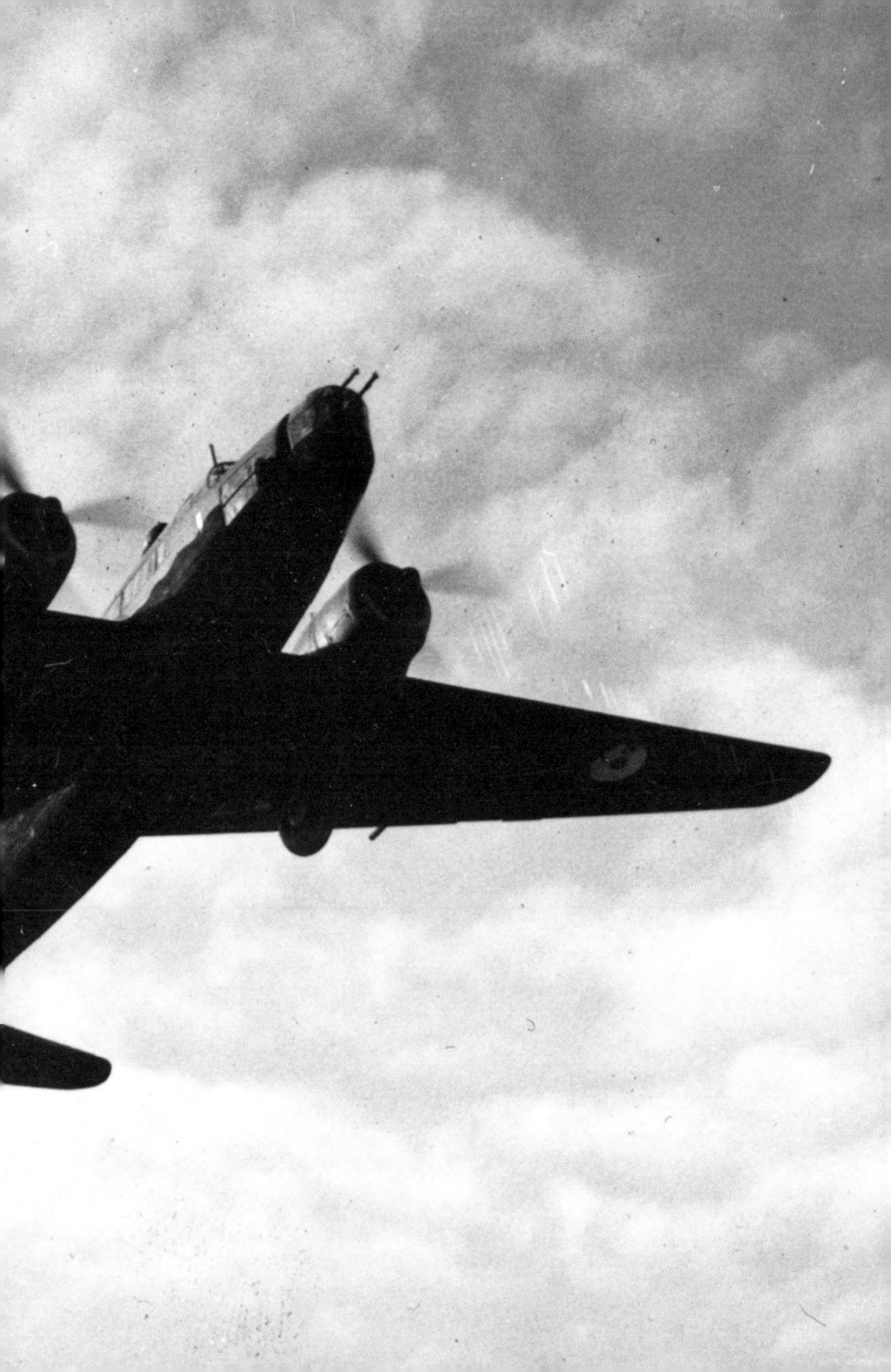

## Civilian Casualties

| | | |
|---|---|---|
| Thomas William Cox | Aged 54 | Landlord of The Chandos Arms |
| William Hawkins | Aged 67 | 4 Rose Cottages |
| Nora Hawkins | Aged 67 | 4 Rose Cottages |
| Israel Goldberg | Aged 67 | 6 Rose Cottages |
| Annie Goldberg | Aged 66 | 6 Rose Cottages |
| Lottie Hoberman | Aged 41 | 6 Rose Cottages - Evacuee |
| Victor Hoberman | Aged 7 | 6 Rose Cottages - Evacuee |
| Stephen Mullis | Aged 35 | 8 Rose Cottages - Home Guard Member |
| Doris Mullis | Aged 39 | 8 Rose Cottages |
| Terence Mullis | Aged 10 | 8 Rose Cottages |
| Kathleen Mullis | Aged 5 months | 8 Rose Cottages |
| Tom Paintin | Aged 55 | 82 High Street |
| Donald Paintin | Aged 18 | 82 High Street - National Fire Service Member |

from Buckingham and Aylesbury and, along with ARP Rescue & Demolition teams, the rescuers worked tirelessly to bring the fires under control. The NFS crews managed to confine the fires to the cottages involved, despite being hampered by exploding ammunition, and prevented any further destruction in the town. The devastation and carnage was appalling, with four crewmen and thirteen civilians being killed. The landlord of the Chandos Arms, Tom Cox, perished as flames engulfed the entire building, but his wife, Helen, survived the destruction of their home. Ironically, Lottie Hoberman and her son, Victor, had been evacuated from their home in Stepney, East London, to escape the terrible bombing of the area. They were living with her parents, Israel and Annie Goldberg, at No.6 Rose Cottages when the Wellington smashed into their home, killing all four occupants.

Miraculously, the navigator, Sgt Jeff Harrison, survived the accident, although he was very seriously injured. Rescuers found a six-month old black and white cat named 'Wimpey', a constant companion and the crew's mascot, tucked into Sgt Harrisons' battle dress blouse and he too had somehow survived the crash.

There were some other miraculous escapes from the destruction that night. One of the aircraft's engines crashed through the roof of a cottage. The occupant, 80 year-old Jack Sawyer, was hurled out of bed by the impact but he still managed to crawl out of the wreckage of his home. At No.8 Rose Cottages

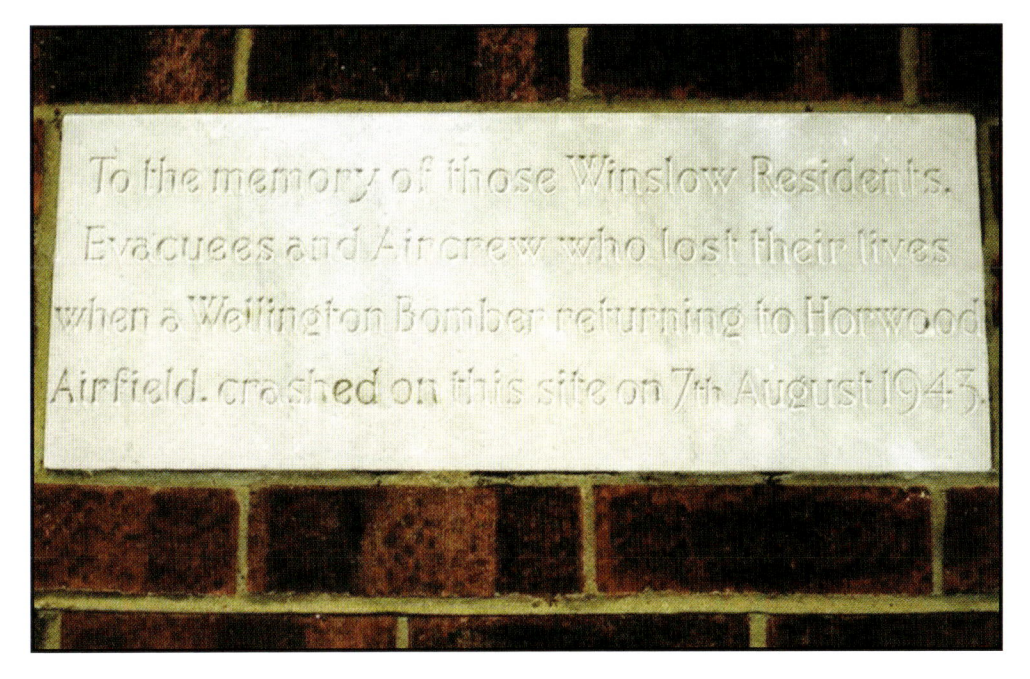

Top: The scene of the crash at The Chandos Arms as it is today
Above: A plaque erected in the memory of those who died that night.

local Home Guard member, Stephen Mullis, his wife and two of his children had perished. However, his two daughters, Sheila aged 11 and June aged 13, managed to jump from the bedroom where they were sleeping into the arms of some servicemen, only suffering slight burns. The cottage in which William and Nora Hawkins lost their lives was now a pile of rubble but rescuers, frantically searching the area, found their six year-old grandson alive and well.

## The Burials

Sgt Davies is buried in the churchyard of Holy Trinity Church, Pontnewydd. Sgt Sowter was cremated at Oxford Crematorium and his ashes were scattered around the lily pond. His name can be found on the services' wall plaque. Sgt McKeon and Sgt Fietz are both buried in the Botley Cemetery, Oxford. On 11th August 1943, Thomas Cox was buried in the Parish Church of Ellesborough, near Aylesbury.

On the same day the bodies of Israel and Annie Goldberg along with Lottie and Victor Hoberman were buried in the Jewish Cemetery in Edmonton, North London. The following day, the remainder of those civilians who perished were buried in the St.Lawrence Churchyard, Winslow.

## The Crash Site Today

As you pass the little parade of shops in the High Street, at the corner of Elmfield Gate, it is hard to imagine the scene of total devastation that must have met the eyes of rescuers and onlookers that night. The site has been totally rebuilt, but if you walk along Elmfield Gate for a few yards you will find the Royal British Legion club and on the wall outside can be seen a memorial tablet to all those who lost their lives in this tragic accident.

Below: The Mullis family grave in Winslow cemetery

# 'MIRIAM' - THE SWEETHEART OF PRINCES RISBOROUGH

## 13th November 1943

**LOCATION**
Longwick, Princes Risborough

**TYPE**
Boeing B-17G Flying Fortress

**SERIAL No.**
42-31038  GY:N 'Miriam'

**UNIT**
367th Bomb Squadron, 306th Bomb Group (Heavy), 8th USAAF

**PILOT**
1st Lieutenant Clyde W COSPER aged 21 – killed

**CREW**
2nd Lieutenant Wesley B BRINKLEY
Co-Pilot – Baled Out
2nd Lieutenant Allen T BALLARD
Navigator – Baled Out
2nd Lieutenant Donald F DICKSON
Bombardier – Baled Out
Technical Sergeant Charles VONDRACHEK
Top Turret Gunner – Baled Out
Sergeant Kenneth IVIEMY
Radio Operator – Baled Out
Staff Sergeant Stanley G DOWNS
Ball Turret Gunner – Baled Out
Staff Sergeant Harold K TWING
Left Waist Gunner – Baled Out
Staff Sergeant Lloyd L MEYER
Right Waist Gunner – Baled Out
Staff Sergeant Denver A McGINNIS
Tail Gunner – Baled Out

On 13th November 1943 twenty-one B-17 Flying Fortresses took off from Thurleigh in Bedfordshire to attack the Kreigsmarine U-boat pens in Bremen, Germany. The weather conditions were very poor and had made the take-off more precarious than usual, and the climb for altitude even worse. The air armada struggled to assemble correctly over the English countryside and, before they reached the coast, it was decided that the mission should be aborted and the crews were told to return to their respective bases. Shortly before they were recalled, B-17G 42-31038, nicknamed 'Miriam', after the pilot's mother, ran into a thunderhead where the downdraft from severe air turbulence caused the fully loaded aircraft to go into a spin, suddenly losing several thousand feet in height in just a few short terrifying seconds. The pilot, 1/Lt Clyde W Cosper, fought with the controls and managed to bring the aircraft into level flight for just long enough to allow his crew to bale out over the Buckinghamshire countryside. 1/Lt Cosper could see that his aircraft was heading directly for the town of Princes Risborough and made heroic efforts to put the stricken plane down in an open field near Summersley Road, on the outskirts of the town. He managed to pull the plane up high enough to clear the rooftops and crashed into a field, well clear of the village. However, the combination of a full load of bombs and fuel meant that moments after striking the ground the aircraft exploded and was blown into pieces. The pilot

*Buckinghamshire* [ 47 ]

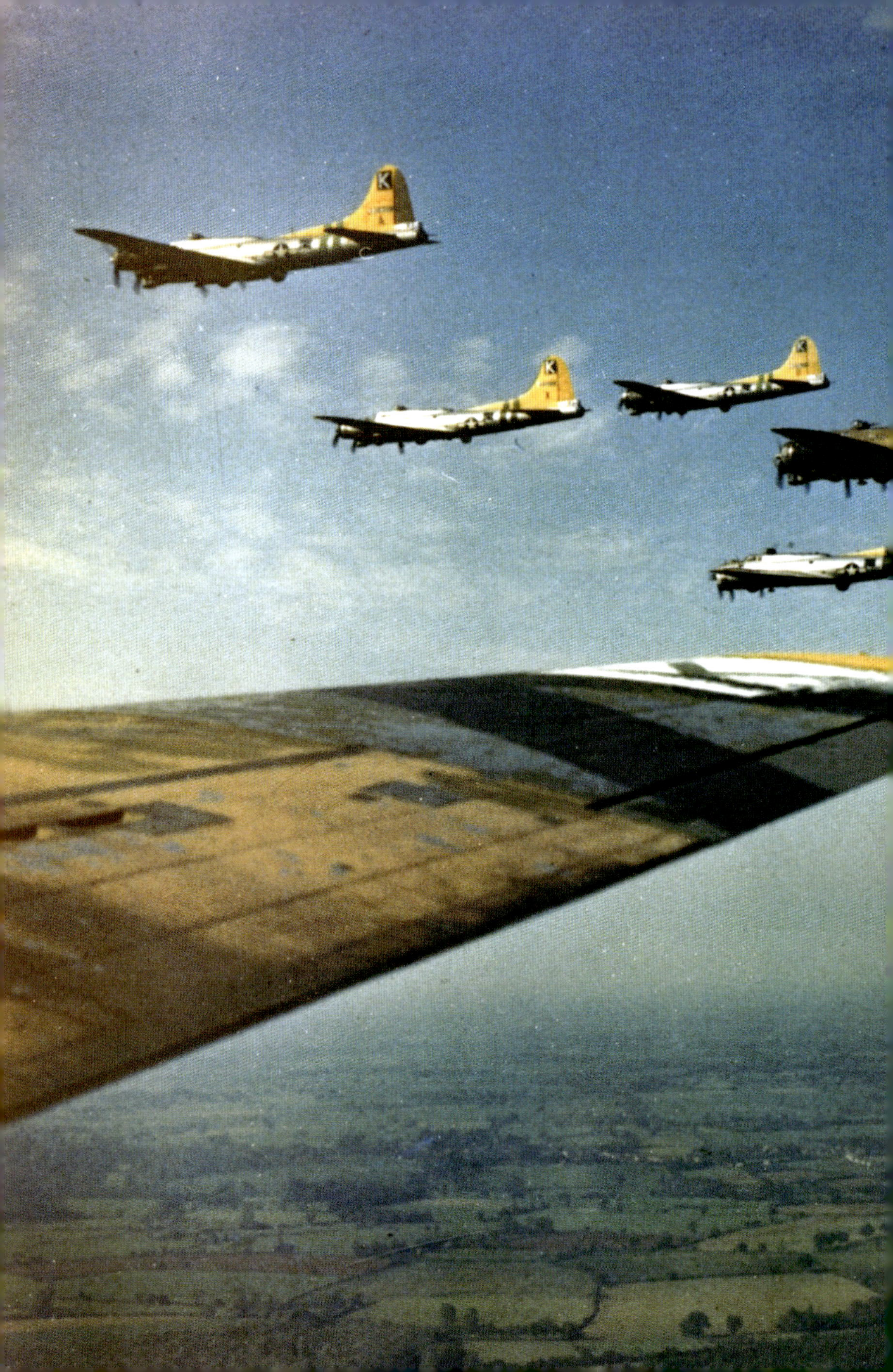

**By winter 1943, the skies above Buckinghamshire were regularly being filled by B-17s of the Eighth Air Force.**

was killed instantly and one nearby resident was pinned inside his milking shed by a piece of the aeroplane's tail, but was otherwise unharmed.

The crew had descended safely and were dispersed around the area. Sadly, the Bombardier, 2/Lt Donald F Dickson, was to lose his life just four weeks later when the B-17 he was flying in was shot down over the North Sea.

At home in Dodd City, Texas, Clyde Cosper's mother, Miriam, received the official telegram informing her of his death. This was a terrible shock from which she never really recovered and in 1954 she took her own life. In 1989 the crash site was excavated and several interesting objects turned up. One of Clyde Cosper's 'Dog Tags' and the metal insignia from his cap. Another item was the intercom switch, which was found to still be in the 'On' position. Originally these artifacts were placed on display at the Booker Aircraft Museum at Wycombe Park. When the museum closed the contents were spread far and wide and it is not known where these items are now.

For his actions that day, Clyde Cosper was awarded the Silver Star, the Distinguished Flying Cross, the Air Medal and the Purple Heart. The incident was all but forgotten by the early 1990s, except by one woman. Maureen Knopp was an 11 year-old at the time of the crash and vividly recalled seeing the stricken B-17 as Clyde Cosper desperately attempted to steer it away from the town. She was determined that the sacrifice made by this young man would not be forgotten. On a cold November day in 1992 her dream came true as a memorial was unveiled to honour the memory of the young American pilot. The man she had never met was etched in her memory as someone who had made the ultimate sacrifice and given his life in a selfless act of heroism. Outside the public library in Princes Risborough stands a modest memorial, the inscription on the plaque dedicated to the lone airman who died all those years ago. Although today the crash site has now been built over, if you walk along one can still visualise the blazing aircraft as it passed over the town and into the history books. In honour of his sacrifice a nursing home was built in his home town. The Clyde W Cosper Texas State Veterans Home opened May 2001. Clyde Cosper is buried in the Dodd City Cemetery, Fannin County, Texas, USA.

**Above: Clyde Cosper and his memorial stone.**

# 1944

# WELLINGTON AT FOX COVERT

### 5th February 1944

**LOCATION**
Fox Covert

**TYPE**
Vickers Wellington X

**SERIAL No.**
JA455

**UNIT**
26 Operational Training Unit
Royal Air Force

**PILOT**
Sergeant Edward Townsend BOWE RAAF aged 20 - injured

**CREW**
Sergeant J CORRIGAN - injured
Sergeant James Scott DUGUID RCAF (Navigator) aged 23 - killed
Flight Sergeant William Clifton KINSMAN RAAF aged 20 - killed
Sergeant Bryan Joseph O'HARE RAAF aged 21 - injured
Sergeant K L PIERCE - uninjured

No.26 Operational Training Unit was formed at Wing on 15th January 1942, equipped with Wellingtons to train much needed bomber crews. It continued to operate until March 1946, during which time many aircrew passed through the airfield gates including Australians and Canadians, who were often thrown together in operational crews as part of the British Commonwealth Air Training Plan. One such crew was that of Sgt Edward Bowe, a young Australian from Sydney.

On the night of 5th February 1944 Sgt Bowe and his crew took off from Wing airfield to perform a training flight. The Wellington was returning to the airfield and was preparing to land when it lost power and crashed at Fox Covert, midway between Wing and Stewkley. In the National Archives you can find a detailed account of the accident, which cost the lives of two of the crew, an Australian and a Canadian. The following is an extract of that report;

*Sgt Bowe on returning from the exercise called base on the R/T at 2305hours. At this time he instructed the Bomb Aimer to switch on the Nacelle tanks and the Bomb Aimer reported that this was done after going to the rear of the aircraft. At 2308 hours he was given instructions to reduce height to 1500 feet, and go over to visual control which he acknowledged. Less than a minute after both engines cut and from eye witnesses accounts Bowe tried to put the aircraft down on the aerodrome. His undercarriage was locked down and approx 28 degrees of flaps down. He lost height, downwind, crossing the left hand boundary close to the runway in use at approx 400 feet and then tried to turn on to the flare path. He did not have sufficient height to execute the necessary turn and the aircraft cashed in Fox Covert 200 yards short of the flare path. The fuel supply to the engines had been cut off. The main fuel supply cocks CP and CS had been turned off by the Bomb Aimer, when the Nacelle tanks should have been turned on. He also had a lack of familiarity with the new type of Nacelle fuel cock.*

Sgt James Duguid and F/Sgt William Kinsman are buried in the Oxford (Botley) Cemetery, UK. Australians, Sgt Edward Bowe and Sgt Bryan O'Hare survived the crash, and the war. Sgt Corrigan and Sgt Pierce also survived the crash but there are no further details of their service.

**Below: The MkX Wellington was the most widely produced version of the type, seeing service with most of the bomber OTUs**

# DUTCH SAILORS OF GAWCOTT

The Netherlands Marineluchtvaartdienst (Naval Air Service) was founded in August 1917 as an independent part of the Royal Dutch Navy. Following the German invasion in May 1940 many of MLD crews managed to escape to England with their Fokker seaplanes. These aircraft served for a short time and the crews played an important role during the war. On 1st June 1940 the famous Dutch 320 Squadron was established at Pembroke Dock in Wales. The squadron started flying their own Fokker aircraft but these were soon replaced by Hudsons and later by B-25 Mitchells. In June 1943 the Dutch 860 Squadron was established in Scotland and operated Swordfish biplanes from aircraft carriers.

It was three members of the MLD who were to be involved in an accident in Buckinghamshire in February 1944.

The aircraft, piloted by CPO Henri Boots, took off from Finmere to carry out circuits and landings as part of their ongoing training. The three airmen had been in the air for about twenty minutes when the aircraft was seen flying at a height of about 500 feet with its starboard engine feathered. An eye witness then described how the machine was skidding from side to side, as though it was in trouble. It began losing height but gaining speed as it disappeared behind a belt of trees near the airfield, whereupon it crashed. A fire broke out immediately on impact and all the crew perished.

## 16th February 1944

**LOCATION**
Gawcott

**TYPE**
North American B-25 Mitchell

**SERIAL No.**
FL194

**UNIT**
13 Operational Training Unit
Royal Air Force

**PILOT**
Pilot Officer David HUDSON
ages 23 – killed

**CREW**
Chief Petty Officer Henri J BOOTS (Pupil Pilot) aged 26 – Royal Dutch Navy – Killed
Sub Lieutenant Henrie J P JANSEN (Pupil Navigator) aged 29 – Royal Dutch Navy – Killed
Petty Officer Jan G E WISSERKERKE (Pupil Air Gunner) aged 21 – Royal Dutch Navy – Killed

P/O David Hudson is buried in Eston Cemetery, Yorkshire. Records for the MLD are seriously lacking and I have not been able to establish the burial locations of the remainder of the crew. It is reasonable to assume that the bodies of Henrie Jansen and Jan Wisserkerke were probably repatriated to the Netherlands after the war. Henri Boots, however, married Mary Sale in Cambridge in the summer of 1943 and it is possible he may be buried in that area.

**Below: A Dutch 320 Squadron crew sit in front of their B-25 Mitchell, note the Dutch orange triangle in the bomb tally.**

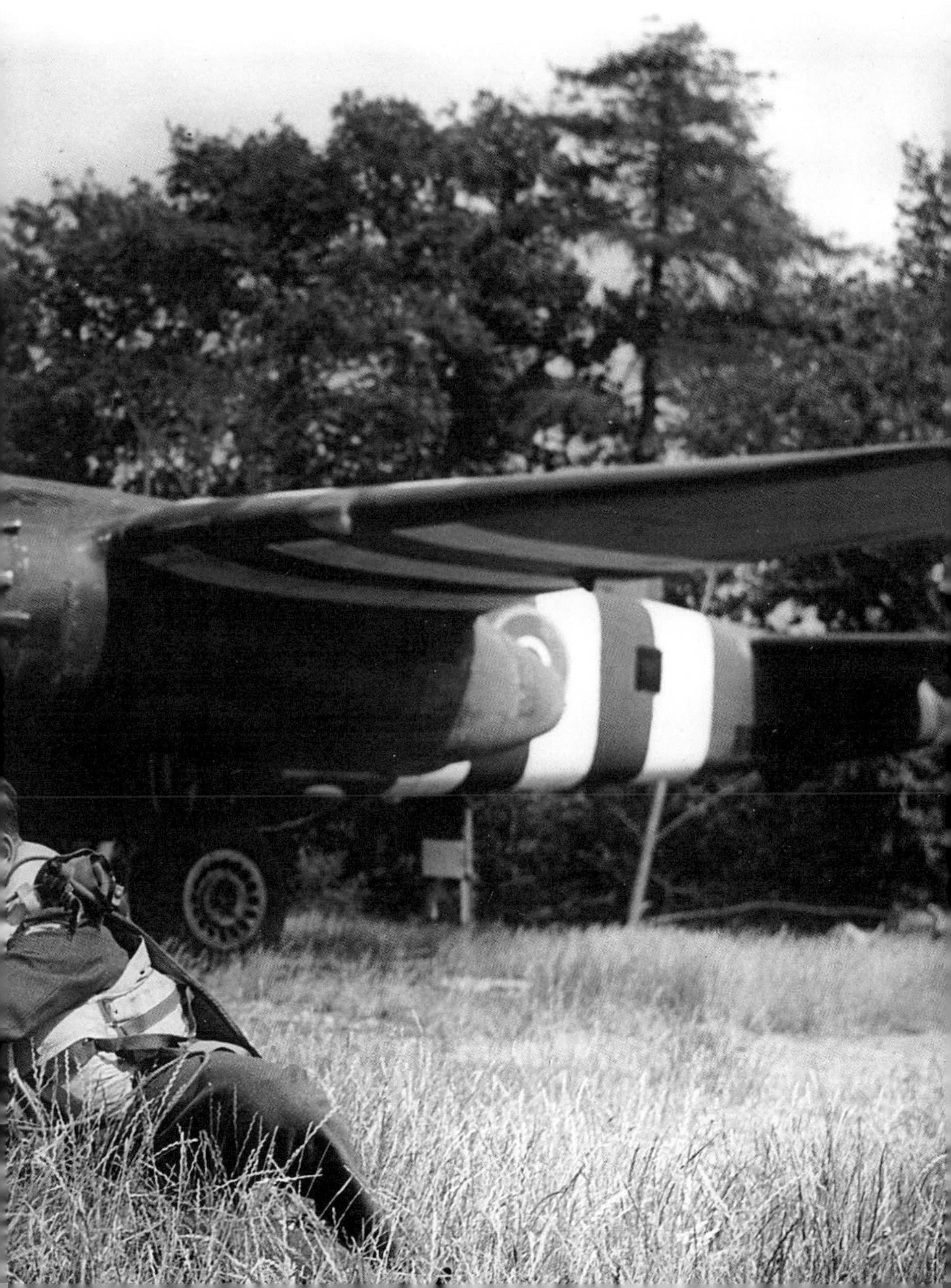

# IT'S COME DOWN ON ANDRIDGE COMMON!!

by Julian Evan Hart

## Combat

This aircraft was engaged on an operation either as a night intruder or, more likely, due to quite heavy raids in this area as a light bomber. It was engaged by gun site SM7 of 564 (M) HAA Battery stationed on Dorney Common. Four 3.7inch AA guns engaged the enemy aircraft that was at an altitude of 11,800 feet and fired a total of 42 rounds. As the AA rounds exploded and flashed close to their target the aircraft banked very sharply, released its bomb load as well as several flares and then proceeded in the direction of High Wycombe. The fact that this aeroplane released flares might have been to try and confuse the defences into thinking it was an Allied aircraft. It is possible that one of the bombs from this aircraft was the one that fell and detonated in a nearby field causing a 12ft by 5ft crater and damaging 50 houses. The aircraft was observed approaching from a southern direction at a very low altitude, with a long streak of flame behind it. Suddenly the engines

### 22-23rd February 1944

**LOCATION**
Henhouse Field, Andridge Farm, Radnage

**TIME**
00:45

**TYPE**
Messerschmitt Me 410A

**CODES**
U5+Q?

**UNIT**
16/KG2

**CREW**
Lieutenant Felix MULLER
aged 34 - killed
Gefreiter Karl-Heinz BOROWSKI
aged 19 - killed

**Above: The Messerchmitt 410 was a fast and agile aircraft often used for hit and run raids over the south coast of England.**

were heard to rev up very sharply and almost immediately after this the aircraft dived into the ground. There was no explosion as it crashed, but wreckage was spread over quite a large area, some of which set fire to a nearby hedge. Parts of the two crew members were found in a neighbouring field to the impact site, having been thrown there by the force of the crash.

The AA Battery Commander, Major Haines, sent a guard party out to the crash site, later they returned in triumph bringing with them one of the propeller blades. This soon took pride of place in a NAAFI canteen party held to celebrate their success. The following morning at the crash site a fragment of W/T operator's briefing sheet was found with call-signs 'Winzer' and 'Hefter' filled in for 16/KG2. On the same document fragment, details including three red visual navigation beacons in the Pas-de-Calais region were also given. According to Eric Higgs, an eyewitness who still lives in Radnage today, during the night a local farmer and his daughter went up to have a look at the crash site and were challenged by the local Home Guard posted around the area. Apparently they refused to answer the challenge or co-operate and ended up nearly being shot before the situation was defused. Eric's father and three Home Guard colleagues had seen the aeroplane scream over on fire and someone said, "It's come down on Andridge Common". Crossing the fields and investigating further they found a propeller blade about 600 yards from the main impact point. As they approached the main crash area they found tattered

**Left and Opposite page:**

The dig in 1971 recovered a significant amount of wreckage icluding some of the cannon armament.

flying boots with feet still in them and a flying glove with a hand still inside it. Two parachutes were located still all 'buckled up'. The next morning the RAF recovery team arrived with a Queen Mary low loader and eventually used this to remove one of the engines and some wreckage which they had dug out. Eric's father noticed that there were many 20mm cannon shells strewn about the crater and picked up a few shreds of metal as souvenirs. Later he would scratch the time date and place on them for posterity, but sadly like many war time trophies they have been lost over the ensuing years. Interestingly when the author spoke to Eric Higgs in March 2008 he mentioned that he believed this German aeroplane had been 'chased all the way from Slough and eventually shot down by fighters'….. it was a great privilege after all these years to now be able to share with Eric the true facts behind that dark night so long ago.

An interesting note to this incident is that the crash slightly damaged a local farmhouse where a young seven year old lad was living. This young lad was Oliver Reed, who later went on to become one of England's legendary film actors. According to his biography he was traumatised by the sight of the body parts from one of the German crewmen.

It was recovered in 1971 by Chiltern Historical Aircraft Preservation Group who unearthed one Daimler Benz DB601 engine, a propeller blade and other parts which were originally placed on display in the Booker Aircraft Museum but now reside in a private collection.

After the 1944 *Operation Steinbock* raids, Luftwaffe incursions against Britain were drastically reduced, becoming token gestures for psychological effect. However in their place came numbers of Hitler's new V weapons, firstly the V-1 or 'Doodlebug' followed shortly by the V-2 the World's first ballistic missile. Both types of weapons fell in Buckinghamshire, but with D-Day and the Allied push into Occupied Europe, these weapons of war petered out slowly until they stopped.

Records show that a total of 27 V-1s fell in Buckinghamshire. One V-1 exploded scattering propaganda leaflets far and wide, an extremely rare incident.

# THE AUSSIE HERO OF QUAINTON

One of the most ironic stories I have come across in my research is that of Flying Officer James Lyon, a young Australian pilot who, along with his crew, perished on the night of 15th March 1944 in a mid-air collision over Buckinghamshire.

### The Pilot

James Henry Scott Lyon was born on 27th June 1922 in Sale, Victoria, Australia. He joined the Royal Australian Air Force on 22nd May 1941 as an Aircraftman and commenced a programme of training that would see him serve with various units in Australia and Rhodesia. Eventually, on 25th August 1942, he was posted to the UK and after a few weeks at a Reception Centre in Bournemouth arrived at No.14 Advanced Flying Unit in Ossington, Nottinghamshire where his training continued. On 12th January 1943 Jim Lyon moved to No.19 Operational Training Unit in Kinloss, Scotland, where he would fly Whitley twin-engined bombers. It was whilst serving in Scotland that he met Margaret Bruce and the couple were to eventually marry at Newark on 23rd November 1943. He returned to Nottinghamshire in March 1943 where he underwent conversion training to the four-engined Lancaster before joining an operational squadron. He finally arrived at RAF Bardney in Lincolnshire in June 1943, where he would serve with No.9 Squadron. Jimmy was to fly a well known Bomber Command Lancaster named 'Spirit of Russia' and he and his crew completed a tour of operations in September of that year. The autumn of 1943 was a busy one for young Jimmy. He moved to RAF

**Above:** FO James Henry Scott Lyon DFC RAAF

## 15th March 1944

### LOCATION

| Quainton | Astwell Park (Northampton) |
|---|---|
| **TYPE** | **TYPE** |
| Vickers Wellington X | Stirling III |
| **SERIAL No.** | **SERIAL No.** |
| LN660 KJ-O | EH989 WP-P |
| **UNIT** | **UNIT** |
| 11 Operational Training Unit, Royal Air Force | 90 Squadron |
| **PILOT** | **PILOT** |
| Flying Officer James Henry Scott LYON RAAF DFC aged 21 - killed | Flight Sergeant Joseph Vernon SPRING aged 22 - killed |
| **CO-PILOT** | **FLIGHT ENGINEER** |
| Flight Sergeant Donald Victor Roy FRANCIS RNZAF aged 24 - killed | Sergeant George Edward COLLINS aged 30 - killed |
| **NAVIGATOR** | **NAVIGATOR** |
| Flying Officer Gerald Harman GILBERT RNZAF aged 23 - killed | Sergeant Thomas Raymond HEWITT aged 23 - killed |
| **AIR BOMBER** | **AIR BOMBER** |
| Pilot Officer Rennie TAYLOR aged 23 - killed | Sergeant John Henry BONE aged 22 - killed |
| **W/OP AIR GUNNER** | **WIRELESS OPERATOR** |
| Flight Sergeant George HUDSON aged 23 - killed | Sergeant Arthur Henry ESTCOURTE aged 29 - killed |
| **W/OP AIR GUNNER** | **MID GUNNER** |
| Sergeant Robert Reginald KEMP aged 20 - killed | Sergeant William Halkett RAMSAY aged 22 - killed |
| **AIR GUNNER** | **REAR GUNNER** |
| Sergeant Reginald Dennis BARLOW aged 21 - killed | Sergeant William BRUCE aged 22 - Killed |
| **AIR GUNNER** | |
| Flight Sergeant Arthur Frederick GOOLD RNZAF aged 21 - killed | |

**Stirling crew members, FSgt Joseph Vernon Spring, Sgt Arthur Henry Estcourte, Sgt George Edward Collins.**

**Below: A 90 Squadron Stirling takes off from Tuddenham.**

Wescott in October to undertake the role of instructor with No.11 Operational Training Unit. He married his sweetheart Margaret, and the couple moved to a rented cottage at 81 Station Rd, Quainton, where they were expecting their first child. In December Jimmy was awarded the Distinguished Flying Cross. The Citation in the London Gazette of 10th December 1943 reads as follows:

*"F/O Lyon has completed, in various capacities, many successful operations against the enemy, in which he has displayed high skill, fortitude and devotion to duty."*

## The Accident

The story begins at 18.50 hours when Stirling III EH989, P-for-Peter, took off from its base at Tuddenham, Suffolk, for a raid on Amiens, France. Flight Sergeant Joseph Spring was at the controls of the massive bomber and was flying with a crew who had only been posted to the squadron a few days before. This was their first operational sortie and one can only imagine the apprehension of those aboard as they headed towards their objective. Although there was intense flak over the target area, night fighter activity was deemed to be fairly negligible and Flight Sergeant Spring and his crew set a course for home. They would never reach their base.

In the meantime, at RAF Westcott in Buckinghamshire, Wellington X LN660 O-for-Orange took off at 20.05 hours to undertake a routine night cross country exercise, a training flight that involved navigational exercises with a fully operational crew. F/O James Lyon, the duty staff instructor, was at the controls. The flight was due to take two-and-a-half hours and was near completion as the Wellington returned to its home base. At 22.35 hours the crew were making their final preparations for landing as they descended out of the clouds towards the airfield. Suddenly, the Wellington was lifted into the air as Stirling EH989 struck it from below and on the starboard side. The Wellington immediately burst into flames and went out of control. A Quainton resident, Jim Bailey, recalled what happened next. He had been working in the railway stations signal box on the night of the crash and recalled seeing the blazing Wellington flying low over Quainton. He believed that F/O Lyon was trying to avoid hitting the station yard, which was full of goods wagons loaded with fuel. The young pilot managed to not only miss the railway yard but also the house in Station Road, Quainton where his pregnant wife was sleeping. Jim Bailey and another witness, Frank Wheeler, watched in horror as the aircraft crashed and exploded in a field near to the railway line.

The crippled Stirling remained airborne for a further 10 to 15 minutes after the collision, calling 'darky' for an emergency landing, but crashed in flames at

**Wellington crew-members L-R, F/O Gerald Harman Gilbert RNZAF, F/Sgt Arthur Frederick Goold, F/Sgt Donald Victor Roy Francis RNZAF, Sgt Robert Reginald Kemp.**

22.47 hours, 17 miles to the north-west at Astwell Park, Northamptonshire, killing all of the crew.

## The Aftermath

An accident investigation report showed that the Stirling was way off course when it struck the Wellington which, after the collision, lost height rapidly. It was too low to allow time for the crew to bale out, the aircraft burst into flames and crashed into a field half a mile east of Quainton Road railway station, one-and-a-half miles north-east of Westcott.

In 1978, following information given to them by Bruce Blanche (F/O Lyon's nephew), the Chiltern Historical Aircraft Preservation Group conducted a six-week dig at the site of the Wellington crash. They uncovered an engine, parachutes and other pieces of the aircraft. Jimmy Lyon was buried with full military honours a few days after the crash at Lennel Old Churchyard in the little town of Coldstream, Berwickshire, in a plot belonging to his young widow's family. On 9th September 1944 his son, Rowland James Lyon, was born at Coldstream.

The Commonwealth War Graves Commission have mis-recorded Joseph Spring's age as 18 on his headstone. A brief search of the national birth records show that he was born in the autumn of 1921 and was, in fact, aged 22 when he died.

P/O Gilbert, F/Sgt Francis and F/Sgt Goold are buried in the Oxford (Bottley) Cemetery. P/O Taylor is buried in the Keighley (Oakworth) Cemetery. F/Sgt Hudson is buried in the Rotherham (Masborough) Cemetery. Sgt Kemp is buried in the Pentney (St Mary Magdalene) Churchyard. Sgt Barlow is buried in the Birmingham (Brandwood End) Cemetery.

# FRIENDLY FIRE AT LITTLE CHALFONT

## 24th March 1944

**LOCATION**
Little Chalfont

**TYPE**
Handley-Page Halifax II

**SERIAL No.**
JD317

**UNIT**
1659 Heavy Conversation Unit

**PILOT**
Flying Officer Martin Stewart LITTLE RCAF aged 23 - killed

**CREW**
Sergeant Derek J WEBB DFM survived
Pilot Officer J S BERESFORD RCAF survived/injured
Sergeant J MACKENZIE RCAF survived/injured
Sergeant N E COWAN RCAF survived/injured

The 24th of March 1944 is a date that holds particular significance in the annals of RAF history. It is recognised as the date of the last of 16 raids on the German capital between November 1943 and March 1944, commonly referred to as the Battle of Berlin. The raids caused immense devastation and loss of life in the city and cost Bomber Command more than 500 precious aircraft. This was also the date on which 76 Allied prisoners-of-war escaped from Stalag Luft III, a German PoW camp in Sagan, Poland that housed captured Allied airmen. Their bold action was the largest mass escape of Allied prisoners during the Second World War and subsequently became the basis for both the book and film 'The Great Escape'.

For two aircrews of No.1659 Heavy Conversion Unit based at RAF Topcliffe in Yorkshire, however, it was business as usual. They were detailed to carry out 'Bullseye' operations as part of their training and one of these was to end in tragic circumstances over Little Chalfont.

Flying Officer Martin Stewart Little had trained as a pilot in Canada, taking an advanced course on Hudsons before going overseas. He duly flew Wellingtons at an OTU, then went to No.1659 Heavy Conversion Unit. By now he had acquired a crew, which included at least one veteran of an earlier tour of operations. On the night of 24/25 March 1944 he was piloting Halifax JD317 with an all-RCAF crew on a 'Bullseye' exercise. An HCU was the last stop before going to a squadron, and a 'Bullseye' was a mock bombing raid towards the end

Buckinghamshire [ 65 ]

of the course, complete with searchlights and flares but without crossing into enemy territory. His 'target' was Bristol, but the Halifax first flew out over the sea, almost to the coast of France, before returning to Britain via Portland Bill.

The aircraft was early over the coast, and Little flew a 'dogleg' course to kill time. However, when he resumed his approach to the target, he flew an entirely wrong course which brought him over Wales. In making corrections he seems to have confused his navigator who thereafter miscalculated prevailing wind direction and speed. Shortly after midnight, the crew spotted searchlights and flares that they took to be the 'Bullseye' area. At 17,000 feet they approached the target, opened the bomb doors, took photographs of their objective, and closed the bomb doors again. The flight engineer, Sergeant Derek Webb, DFM, then described what happened:

*"Just as we closed the bomb doors, flak started bursting all round us and one burst went through the wing just behind the port outer engine. I immediately fired the colours of the day. The skipper put on his navigation lights and downward identification light. The starboard inner engine was then hit and the pilot said he was losing control and gave the order to bale out. I continued to fire the colours of the day, 5 in all, until I had none left. I then put the skipper's parachute pack on him and fired the three red distress cartridges we had. By this time the other engines had all been hit and the aircraft was definitely diving. The navigator and bomb aimer were out and the wireless operator just going out. The two gunners were waiting at the front hatch to bale out, after the wireless operator. I realised that I had a poor chance of getting out if I waited until the two gunners left as the aircraft was then at 8,000 feet. I went to the back of the aircraft and baled out the rear escape hatch at approximately 0050 hours."*

It was not, however, a 'friendly fire' incident as usually understood. JD317, hopelessly off track, had flown into the London defence zone at the precise moment that the Luftwaffe was mounting its last raid on the British capital. The red flares the Canadians had seen were, in fact, German target indicators; the searchlights were British, looking for a real enemy and the Halifax was making what appeared on the radar to be a bombing run. Unlike a 'Bullseye' exercise, there were real guns firing real proximity-fused shells, directed by the latest radar. After his crew had baled out Flying Officer Little remained at the controls of the stricken bomber. It would appear that it was too late for him to leave the aircraft safely and he was praised for steering it away from 'a village' and saving his crew but losing his own life. The aircraft crashed at Lodge

Farm, south-east of Little Chalfont. Three members of crew were admitted to hospitals at Amersham and Watford suffering from sprains and shock.

## The Investigation

A subsequent Court of Enquiry found that there was some dispute as to whether the aircraft's IFF (Identification, Friend or Foe) had been switched on, and if so, whether it was operable. Only one witness on the ground reported seeing the colours of the day fired, and these were the wrong colours. It appears that the distress flares were, understandably, mistaken for German flares. There was an unusually strong northerly wind which, along with the navigator's misjudgment, had taken the Halifax over 100 miles off course and into the London Zone. Sadly, through a series of errors, JD317 had wound up at the wrong place at the worst possible time.

## The Crash Site Today

The crash site location can be found after you go under the railway bridge in Lodge Lane from the Amersham-Rickmansworth Road and at the bend in the road after the dip. It was on the left just before the Long Walk turning that an eyewitness, at the time, recalled seeing wreckage stuck in the trees. If you visit this site, spare a thought for F/O Martin Little who lays buried in the Canadian plot at Brookwood Military Cemetery, Surrey.

## Postscript

When carrying out any form of historical research it is vital, for the benefit of future generations, that any statements made are as factually correct as possible. During my research into this particular accident it has become apparent that a number of well-intentioned individuals have made claims that this aircraft was returning to its base after having been involved in a diversionary attack that took place to the west of Paris in support of the Berlin raid. This is not the case. It was on a training flight that had no involvement in the operation to Berlin. Some publications also only list the names of the pilot and the three injured crewmen. In fact, there was a full crew of seven aboard and it was F/O Martin Little who laid down his life for them and the people of Little Chalfont. Remember him.

# THE ANGELS OF WING

The airfields of Britain were in a state of heightened activity in June 1944, following the D-Day landings on the beaches of Normandy. Despite the high level of operational flights that were taking place there was need to ensure that training flights were maintained. On the evening of 9th June 1944 a Wellington of No.26 OTU took off from Wing airfield at 16.45 hours to carry out a standard night flying exercise, with two crew members aboard, F/O Richard Huband and F/O Harry Wilkes DFM. Just ten minutes after leaving the ground the aircraft smashed into the airfield and burst into flames destroying another Wellington X, HE786, and a Tomahawk IIb, AK116, which was loaded on a Queen Mary transporter, parked near No.4 Hanger. Sadly, as well as the two aircrew, three WAAFs of No.71 Maintenance Unit were also caught in the resulting explosion. LACW Mary Conway and LACW Ann Reeves, died on the ground. ACW1 Emily Dickens was badly injured and died the next day.

The cause of the accident was never determined, but what is known is that F/O Huband had been involved in an accident on 20th June 1943 in which he and a Canadian, P/O Charles Woodley, made a forced landing at night after an engine on their Wellington cut out a short while after taking off from RAF Wing. On the day before Huband died, Woodley was killed on operations whilst

| 9th June 1944 | |
|---|---|
| LOCATION | Wing |
| TYPE | Vickers Wellington X |
| SERIAL No. | HE854 |
| UNIT | 26 Operational Training Unit, Royal Air Force |
| PILOT | Flying Officer Richard Francis HUBAND aged 22 - killed |
| CREW | Flying Officer Harry WILKES DFM aged 23 - killed |
| CASUALTIES ON THE GROUND | Leading Aircraftswoman Mary Jane CONWAY aged 25 - killed<br>Leading Aircraftswoman Ann Alice Minnie REEVES aged 21 - killed<br>Aircraftswoman 1st Class Emily Marjorie DICKENS aged 22 - died of wounds |

flying with No.15 Squadron over France. Perhaps the loss of a close friend was too much to bear.

F/O Harry Wilkes had been awarded the Distinguished Flying Medal on 26th November 1943 whilst serving as a Sergeant with 150 Squadron. The recommendation from his Commanding Officer reads as follows;

*"Sergeant Wilkes joined the Squadron on the 14th June 1943, and has since flown 40 sorties involving 253 operational hours against the enemy in Tunisia, Sicily and Italy. He has Captained his crew well and has fostered an excellent team spirit. He was always keen to be attacking the enemy and has done brilliant work in pressing home attacks on the enemy's evacuation beaches at Cap Bon. Many of these attacks were at low level against well defended targets, but Sergeant Wilkes always secured good photographs showing that he had effectively bombed the target. His work in the Squadron also included attacks in support of the landing of troops in Sicily and here, where precision bombing of a high order was required, he acquitted himself well. For his great devotion to duty, exceptional keenness and untiring energy, I recommend Sergeant Wilkes for the D.F.M."*

Above; the pilot's grave at Fladbury.

Below; A Wellington MkX similar to the one that crashed at Wing.

Emily Dickens is buried in Dunstable Cemetery, Bedfordshire. Mary Conway is buried in Redcar Cemetery, Yorkshire and Ann Reeves is buried in Camberwell Cemetery, London. F/O Richard Huband is buried in the St. John The Baptist Churchyard, Fladbury, Worcestershire and F/O Harry Wilkes is buried in the St. Mary Churchyard, Frampton-on-Severn, Gloucestershire.

# 1945

# THE BEAST OF BOURBON

**Above; The Beast of Bourbon with its flamboyant nose-art.**

The USAAF took over Cheddington Airfield for a second time in August 1943 with Consolidated B-24D Liberator bombers of the Combat Crew Reinforcement Centre. November 1944 saw the arrival of a specialist USAAF Radio Counter Measures unit, 36th Bomb Squadron (RCM). The men of this unit flew special operations in modified B-17s and B-24s to jam the German radar controlling the Luftwaffe fighters and flak batteries. They undertook many night missions with the Royal Air Force as well as daylight

## 19th February 1945

**LOCATION**
Cheddington

**TYPE**
Consolidated B-24H Liberator

**SERIAL No.**
42-50385  R4*H 'Beast Of Bourbon'

**UNIT**
36th Bomb Squadron, (Radio Countermeasures), 801st Bomb Group, 8th USAAF

**PILOT**
1st Lieutenant Louis J McCARTHY
injured

**CREW**
2nd Lieutenant Victor E PREGEANT III
injured
2nd Lieutenant John D HOWARTH
injured
2nd Lieutenant James K SNODDY
injured
Staff Sergeant James C. GRIFFITH
injured
Staff Sergeant Robert P. McADAM
injured
Staff Sergeant Richard B. JACKSON
injured
Staff Sergeant H PARKE - Radio Operator
injured
Staff Sergeant Fred K. BECKER
aged 24 - Gunner - killed
Staff Sergeant Howard F. HALEY
aged 21 - Gunner - killed
Staff Sergeant Carl E. LINDQUIST
aged 22 - Gunner - killed

raids with the Eighth Air Force. Their first jamming mission on the morning of D-Day contributed to the success of the landings on the beachhead. The squadron often flew days when bad weather kept the rest of the Eighth Air Force on the ground. Before the war in Europe ended the 36th Bomb Squadron had flown 220 operations to stop the enemy from learning important mission details.

On the night of 19th February 1945 a B-24H Liberator, nicknamed 'Beast of Bourbon', piloted by Lt Louis McCarthy, took off from Station 113 at Cheddington in very poor weather conditions. The pilot, who could only make use of his instruments for guidance, was also giving Lt Victor E. Pregeant III, a new navigator to the squadron from Ponchatoula, Louisiana, a 'check-ride' in preparation for a later operational mission. As the aircraft lifted off from Runway 26 it struck some hedges and trees. McCarthy struggled to keep 'The Beast' under control, but only half a mile west of the runway the Liberator came down just missing a row of cottages in the village of Long Marston. The B-24 ploughed through two hedges, crossed Astrope Lane, then took out two trees before coming to rest in the centre of a field being used for cattle grazing where four cows were shot dead by the exploding .50 calibre machine gun bullets.

**Above: 1st Lieutenant Louis J McCarthy and his crew.**

**Standing left to right** - S/Sgt. James C. Griffith, 2d Lt. John D. Howarth, 1st Lt. Louis J. McCarthy, 2d Lt. James K. Snoddy, S/Sgt. Robert P. McAdam.

**Kneeling left to right** - S/Sgt. Howard F. Haley, S/Sgt. Carl E. Lindquist, S/Sgt. Fred K. Becker, S/Sgt. Richard B. Jackson.
*(via Stephen Hutton, author of Squadron of Deception.)*

Navigator 1/Lt John Howarth managed to scramble out of the wreckage and run to safety but quickly returned to get his crewmates out. He knew it was very risky but he had to do it. Sadly, a few minutes later the B-24 caught fire with three of the crew still trapped inside. They perished in their plane and the aircraft, with its flamboyant nose art, was a total loss. John Howarth carried this enduring memory with him for the remainder of his life.

The dead crewmen were originally buried in the American Military Cemetery in Cambridge. S/Sgt Haley was reinterred at Fort Snelling National Cemetery, South Minneapolis, Minnesota on 5th August 1948. S/Sgt Becker was reinterred at Fort Rosecrans National Cemetery, San Diego, California. S/Sgt Lindquist is known to have been reinterred in Illinois.

# DISTINGUISHED FLYERS COLLIDE

On the afternoon of 6th April 1945 a Wellington Mk.X, HE928, took off from RAF Wing in order to carry out high level bombing practice over the Hogshaw ranges. Pilot Officer Douglas Wix DFC was at the controls and would have been aware that other aircraft would be leaving the airfield to carry out a similar task. Dix had been awarded the Distinguished Flying Medal in June 1942 whilst serving with 144 Squadron. Ninety minutes later Flight Lieutenant Marcel 'Slim' Hore DFC, a New Zealander, also took off from the airfield tasked with the same exercise. Hore, a former banker from Whangarei, North Auckland, was piloting another Wellington Mk.X, LN540, and had a full crew aboard, one of whom, Warrant Officer John Muir, had recently been awarded the Distinguished Flying Medal whilst serving with 51 Squadron. A short time after F/Lt Hore had taken off F/Lt Dix was preparing to bring his aircraft down through the clouds over Winslow. As he did so the two Wellingtons collided and broke up in mid-air with burning wreckage being scattered over a very wide area, as far afield as Sandhill, Verney Junction, Middle Claydon and Mount Pleasant. One of the engines, having buried itself underground, was dug up after being located in the middle of a field on a farm and took two days to unearth.

F/Lt Douglas Wix, who was awarded the DFC on the 26th June 1942, is buried in the St. Mary Church Cemetery, Shinfield, Berkshire. F/Lt Marcel Hore, who was awarded the DFC on the 23rd March 1945 whilst serving with 149 Squadron, lays buried in the Botley Cemetery, Oxford.

## 6th April 1945

**LOCATION**

Winslow

| | |
|---|---|
| **TYPE** | **TYPE** |
| Wellington X | Wellington X |
| **SERIAL No.** | **SERIAL No.** |
| HE928 | LN540 |
| **UNIT** | **UNIT** |
| 26 Operational Training Unit, Royal Air Force | 26 Operational Training Unit, Royal Air Force |
| **PILOT** | **PILOT** |
| Flight Lieutenant Douglas Louis WIX DFC aged 29 - killed | Flight Lieutenant Marcel Launcelot HORE DFC RNZAF aged 23 - killed |
| **NAVIGATOR** | **2ND PILOT** |
| Sergeant Robert James BORLAND aged 20 - killed | Sergeant Derrick John ROWSON aged 20 - killed |
| **BOMB AIMER** | **NAVIGATOR** |
| Sergeant Albert BRIERLEY aged 21 - killed | Sergeant Ernest Walter JENNINGS aged 22 - killed |
| **WIRELESS OP** | **BOMB AIMER** |
| Flight Sergeant Victor Arnold THOMPSON aged 21 - killed | Sergeant Frank Ernest JORDAN aged 22 - killed |
| | **BOMB AIMER** |
| | Warrant Officer John MUIR DFM aged 23 - killed |
| | **WIRELESS OP** |
| | Sergeant Michael Guy Burnett JAMES aged 20 - killed |
| | **AIR GUNNER** |
| | Sergeant Eric Edward BARFOOT aged 19 - killed |

# DOUBLE SACRIFICE AT TAPLOW

## 20th April 1945

**LOCATION**
Popes Field, Taplow

**TYPE**
Lockheed Hudson V

**SERIAL No.**
AM854

**UNIT**
ATA Training Flight. White Waltham

**PILOT**
Third Officer Lesley Cairns MURRAY (Air Transport Auxilliary) aged 28 - killed

**CREW**
Cadet Geoffrey Bernard REGAN (Air Training Corps) aged 16 - killed

At the beginning of 1939 the Horton Kirby Flying Club in Kent saw the formation of the Civil Air Guard Training Unit under the direction of George William Alexander, a former Imperial Airways pilot. It was the aim of the CAG to train a nucleus of civilian pilots through flying clubs and schools. The clubs had to undertake that CAG members would not pay more than ten shillings per hour for training on standard machines. Flying instruction commenced on 10th March 1939 with a fleet of aircraft and nine instructors. Training was continuous. In fine weather at weekends and evenings aircraft would taxi back and without stopping the engine the next pupil would be quickly bundled into the rear cockpit and away they would go for another training session. It was under this scheme that Lesley Murray gained her Pilot's Certificate, number 19125, on 18th July 1939. Sadly, George Alexander was later killed whilst flying a Wellington bomber in a raid on Berlin in 1942.

Lesley Murray commenced flying training with the ATA in June 1943. In July 1944 she undertook a conversion course in order that she could fly the twin-engined Oxford and had acquired a total of 507 hours of flying training by

April 1945 when she was posted to White Waltham for training on the heavier twin Hudson.

## The Accident

On 20th April 1945 Lesley Murray was given fifty minutes tuition by her instructor on piloting a Hudson aircraft, which concentrated on how to perform turning and landing on one engine. Finally, she was given the authority to carry out a solo flight, along with Cadet Geoffrey Regan. Despite his young age Regan was employed by the ATA at White Waltham, as a pilot's authorised assistant. His job was to lower the undercarriage manually should it become necessary and it was a job he had done in the past. A short while after the Hudson left the ground, during which time it should have been flying on one engine, it was seen to be flying at a height of 800-1,000 feet when it turned to the right and immediately drop its nose, after which it went into a fast right hand spin. The aircraft continued in its downward spiral until it slammed into the ground at Popes Field on the outskirts of Taplow, killing both occupants.

Lesley Murray was considered to be a careful and capable pilot and her instructor spoke highly of her abilities. Despite this, the accident was believed to have been caused by the pilot's limited knowledge of this type of aircraft.

Cadet Geoffrey Regan is buried in the London Road Cemetery, Staines, Middlesex and Lesley Cairns is buried in the Chislehurst Cemetery, Kent.

DOUBLE SACRIFICE AT TAPLOW

Above; The cramped cockpit of a Hudson. Lesley Murray had just 50 minutes' instruction on this type before her fatal flight.

Background photo ; A Hudson takes off from an airfield in England.

# AND STILL THEY FELL
## ACCIDENTS POST WW2

# A SWALLOW OVER LITTLE BRICKHILL

## 15th February 1950

**LOCATION**
Little Brickhill

**TYPE**
de Havilland 108 Prototype

**SERIAL No.**
VW120

**UNIT**
Royal Aircraft Establishment

**PILOT**
Squadron Leader John Stuart MULLER-ROWLAND DSO, DFC & Bar aged 28 - killed

### The Aircraft

The de Havilland DH108, unofficially nicknamed the 'Swallow' by the Ministry of Supply, was an experimental aircraft designed by John Carver Meadows Frost in October 1945 and was the first British aircraft to exceed Mach 1. It featured a tailless, swept wing design closely resembling the Messerschmitt Me163 Komet rocket-powered interceptor which was built by the Germans in WW2. The Swallow was developed to explore the effects of high speed flight close to the speed of sound and was built at the de Havilland factory in Hatfield using a standard Vampire fuselage. Three prototypes were built and all of them were to be lost in fatal crashes. There was TG306 which suffered a catastrophic structural failure at 10,000 feet and crashed in the Thames Estuary on 27th September 1946, killing the pilot Geoffrey de Havilland Jnr. The second one was TG283 which crashed on 1st May 1950 whilst carrying out stalling trails at Hartley Wintney, killing the pilot George Genders AFC DFM, when, after abandoning the aircraft at low altitude his parachute failed to open in time. Lastly, there was VW120 which crashed on 15th February 1950 whilst involved in dive research at Little Brickhill, Buckinghamshire, killing the pilot Squadron Leader Stuart Muller-Rowland DSO, DFC & Bar.

The test flight was due to examine the effects of change from sub-sonic to transonic flight, but the aircraft broke up whilst in a high speed dive. During the initial accident investigation witnesses spoke of hearing an explosion but it is not clear if this was the sound of the aircraft breaking up or a sonic boom.

Investigators believed that evidence pointed to a faulty oxygen system that incapacitated the pilot. This, however, is not thought to be the case as a later coroner's report suggests that the pilot may have died from a broken neck due to the violent sideways G forces placed on him when the aircraft lost its port wing during the dive. Wreckage was spread over a wide area with some of it coming down at Little Brickhill. The cockpit was found near to Bow Brickhill church and some other pieces were found as far away as Husborne Crawley. The pilot's body, and one wing, crashed into the ground after striking a tree near Sandy Lane between Bow Brickhill and Woburn Lane on the edge of what is now the Woburn golf complex.

### The Pilot

During the Second World War John Muller-Rowland flew Bristol Blenheim bombers with No.60 Squadron in India, carrying out attacks against Japanese targets in Burma until May 1943. He was awarded the Distinguished Flying Cross on the 8th January 1943, the citation read;

**Above Right; Squadron Leader John Stuart Muller-Rowland.**

**Below; The de Havilland 108 was the first British aircraft to go through the sound barrier.**

*"Flying Officer Muller-Rowland has made many reconnaissances deep into Burma and brought back information of great value. On two occasions recently, he participated in low level attacks against enemy shipping off Akyab. Despite strong opposition from air and ground defences this officer pressed home his attack with great determination. He has proved himself to be a splendid leader and has set a fine example to his fellow pilots".*

On 8th October 1943 he moved to No.211 Squadron in Burma to fly Bristol Beaufighters. He went on to command the squadron between August and October 1944 and was awarded the Distinguished Service Order on 21st November 1944. After the war, with the rank of Squadron Leader, he joined the Empire Test Pilot's School and, after completing No. 6 course, was posted to the Royal Aircraft Establishment in 1948.

**Above; The remains of the rear fuselage of VW120 near Little Brickhill.**

### The Muller-Rowland Tragedy

The tragic loss of a child is something that many of us would find unimaginable. For Daisy Muller-Rowland the pain of such loss was to be three fold. During the Second World War her three sons, Eric, John and Stanley saw distinguished service in the Royal Air Force. In June 1943 during an operational flight off of Sardinia with No.144 Squadron, 26 year-old F/O Eric Muller-Rowland disappeared, his body having never been recovered. Then in October 1944 her youngest son, 23 year-old W/Cdr Stanley Muller-Rowland, disappeared off of the coast of Holland during an operational flight with No.236 Squadron, his body too was never recovered and his name is recorded on the Runnymede Memorial in Surrey. Despite the tragic loss she suffered it must have been a great relief to see her middle son survive his service in the Far East and return home. One can only imagine her feelings when he was then lost in this unfortunate accident. Today when you approach the war memorial in the Surrey village of Horsell you will find the names of Eric and Stanley inscribed upon the tablet honouring the dead of WW2. Sadly, you will not see the name of John as his loss was not as a result of war service.

# BOMBS AND ROCKETS IN BUCKINGHAMSHIRE

### Luftwaffe Air Raids

*Throughout the Second World War Buckinghamshire suffered numerous attacks by the Luftwaffe, due mainly to its proximity to London. Although a majority of raids were carried out by large groups of aircraft, occasionally single aircraft also made lone raids, either in a desperate attempt to dump their payloads and return to their bases, or whilst making 'hit and run' sneak attacks on random targets before they encountered the fighters of the RAF. In Buckinghamshire alone, between 3rd September 1940 and 30th November 1942, a total of 21 men, 18 women and 5 children lost their lives to 'Enemy Action'. In addition, there were a further 123 men, 66 women and 9 children who were injured in the same incidents. There is not provision within this publication to record every incident, but I have highlighted those air raids where there was loss of life inflicted upon both civilians and servicemen alike. Civilians who died as a result of enemy action during the Second World War are commemorated differently than those that died as a result of military service. Their names are recorded on the Civilian War Dead Roll of Honour located in St George's Chapel in Westminster Abbey and their individual records can be found on the Commonwealth War Grave Commission website and in the record books held at the National Archives*

## 15th November 1940

**LOCATION**
Beachampton

The following people died at Elmer's Charity Cottages, Nash Road, Beachampton when the area was hit by a German raider on the night of the 15th/16th November 1940.

| | | |
|---|---|---|
| Minnie Alderman | Aged 60 | Wife of William John Alderman. Died at Elmer's Charity Cottages |
| William John Alderman | Aged 60 | Husband of Minnie Alderman. Died at Elmer's Charity Cottages |
| Lizzie Bennett | Aged 87 | Died at Elmer's Charity Cottages |
| Annie Pearcey | Aged 78 | Widow of A. Pearcey. Died at Elmer's Charity Cottages |

# THE VENGEANCE WEAPONS

The German V-weapons, short for Vergeltungswaffen (retaliation weapon), comprised of the V-1 flying bomb, the V-2 rocket and the V-3 cannon. All of these weapons were intended for use in a military campaign against Britain, though, in the event, only the V-1 and V-2 were ever used. The V-weapon offensive began on the 13th June 1944 and did not come to an end until 29th March 1945. In terms of casualties, their effects had been less than their inventors had hoped, or their victims feared. Property damage was extensive with over 20,000 houses a day being damaged at the height of the campaign, causing a massive housing crisis in south-east England in late 1944 and early 1945.

## The V-1

The Fieseler Fi 103, better known as the V-1, was an early pulse-jet-powered missile. Designed by Lusser and Gosslau, it had a fuselage constructed mainly of welded sheet steel and wings built of plywood. The simple pulse jet engine pulsed fifty times per second and the characteristic buzzing sound gave rise to the nicknames 'buzz bomb' or 'doodlebug'. The launch sites for the V-1 were constructed in Northern France, along the coast from Calais to Le Havre. Aerial bombing attacks on these sites by the Allied air forces were only partially successful and by June 1944 they were ready for action. Following the D-Day landings in Normandy the Germans opted to launch an assault on Britain and, early on the morning of 13th June 1944, the first V-1 flying bomb attack was carried out on London. A total of 9,251 V-1s were fired at Britain with the vast majority being aimed at London. The following is an extract from the incident list held in the county archives.

Opposite Top; A V-1 flying bomb photographed shortly after take-off.

Opposite Below; The V-1 was very difficult to shoot down due to its small size and speed. However, the RAF and the anti-aircraft gun crews eventually worked out tactics to combat the menace, resulting in many V-1s being brought down before reaching their target. This one came down remarkably intact in a field.

THE VENGEANCE WEAPONS

Buckinghamshire

**2nd July 1944**

**LOCATION**
Chestnut Lane, Chesham Bois

At 10.54am on 2nd July 1944 the silence of a quite Sunday morning was shattered as a V-1 flying bomb, whose original target had been London, roared towards Chesham Bois. As the rocket sped across the Buckinghamshire countryside it was fired upon by anti-aircraft guns on the ground. Suddenly, the flying bomb was hit by gunfire and the pulse jet engine popped to an abrupt halt. The rocket began to hurtle earthward and slammed into a house in Chestnut Lane and detonated, the resulting explosion turning the home instantly into a pile of smouldering rubble. The house, named 'Red Leys', was the home of Sir Arthur Scott, a distinguished veteran of both the Boer War and World War One. The district engineer, Mr. R.E.Harris, quickly arrived at the scene to find around 200 people, including Air Raid Wardens, members of the National Fire Service, military and rescue personnel working on the perimeter of the completely collapsed building, which was nothing more than a heap of debris. The Incident Officer, Sgt Biggs, reported that rescue personnel on site were attempting to rescue a trapped casualty and further parties from Missenden and Chesham had been sent for. Harris quickly took stock of the situation and immediately organised the eager workers into chains, there being about 10 chains of approximately 15 men. By mid-day the rescue party had reached a trapped female casualty, this was 18 month-old Christina Hanbury-Sparrow, and a doctor administered a dose of morphine. She was quickly removed and despatched to hospital in a very serious condition, but sadly died as a result of her injuries.

There seemed to be some doubt about the possibility of other casualties, so work was quickly ceased in order that 'listening' could be carried out at various points. A message was sent to the hospital to confirm that there was a further casualty. Lady Scott confirmed that her husband was in the house and was able to give his approximate whereabouts. The rescue party proceeded to search in this part of the debris and a few minutes later located Sir Arthur Scott, trapped in a pancake collapse. It took about 25 minutes to release him, but he was found to be dead. Sadly, the rescuers also discovered the body of Christina Conway amongst the debris.

In all there were 20 casualties, including 3 dead, all of whom had been evacuated in a little more than 1½ hours from the time the V-1 fell, a fact that was considered to be very satisfactory under the circumstances. The rescue personnel proceeded to cover the roofs of damaged properties with tarpaulins, and they continued with this work until 19.00 hours when they were dismissed, due to extreme tiredness. The work of covering the damaged roofs then passed to numerous building contractors. One house, 'Red Leys', was completely demolished, four others were partly demolished and 135 others were damaged in some shape or form. The work of the rescue parties was considered efficient and, although the eager workers of the other services also did excellent work, it was uncontrolled. It was felt that a quick re-organisation of the labour could have been made. A detailed report of the incident and the action that was taken to rescue people can be found in the Buckinghamshire Archives. (ref AR 59/90).

| Civilians who died in this incident | |
|---|---|
| Sir Arthur Scott | Aged 80 |
| Christina Conway | Aged 25 |
| Christina Amelie Hanbury-Sparrow | Aged 18 months |

## A Note On Lt Col. Alan Arthur Hanbury-Sparrow

Lt Col Alan Hanbury-Sparrow went to France in August 1914 with the 1st Battalion of the Berkshire Regiment and was wounded in November 1914. After recovering from his wound he returned to France as second-in-command of the 2nd Battalion. He was wounded again at Pallas Trench in March 1917, invalided to England and returned, eventually to command the 2nd Battalion, only to be severely gassed at Third Ypres in November 1917. It was whilst he was recovering from this injury that he married Eileen Margaret Gray on 27th December 1917. The couple had six children, but eventually divorced in 1937. After recovering from this injury he went on to command the 4th Wiltshire Regiment. He recounted his experiences in his book 'The Landlocked Lake' published in 1932. In 1939 Arthur, now aged 47, married Amelie Roder and in 1942 their daughter, Christina, was born.

# WHISPERING DEATH
# A V2 STRIKES WITHOUT WARNING

### The V-2

The V-2 rocket, designed by Wernher Magnus Maximilian von Braun, was first conceived in early 1936 and was the world's earliest ballistic missile. In October 1942 the first fully operational model was launched from Peenemunde, Germany and reached an altitude of sixty miles, becoming the first rocket to reach the fringes of space. During 1943/44 the Germans built secret launching sites in Northern France but these were quickly overrun by the Allies following the D-Day invasions. Alternative launching sites were set up around The Hague in Holland and the first offensive rocket was launched from there against London on 8th September 1944. It took an estimated five minutes to fly the 200 miles to London where it smashed to earth in Chiswick, causing thirteen casualties. By October 1944 the offensive had become sustained and intercepting the supersonic missiles in flight proved impossible.

Other counter measures, such as bombing the launch sites, were also fairly ineffectual. Sustained bombardment by the V-2s continued until 27th March 1945 when one of the last V-2 missiles to be launched hit a block of flats in Stepney, killing 134 people and injuring 49. 1,115 V-2s were fired at the United Kingdom killing an estimated 2,754 civilians and a further 2,917 service personnel. Two fell in Buckinghamshire.

A V-2, launched from The Hauge, exploded in Stoke Poges causing considerable damage to housing and some casualties.

**11th February 1945**

LOCATION
Stoke Poges

A V2, launched from The Hauge, exploded in Iver Heath causing considerable damage to housing and some casualties.

**15th February 1945**

LOCATION
Iver Heath

Background photo; The V-2 rocket, a truly terrifying weapon.

# BUCKINGHAMSHIRE INCIDENT & ACCIDENT LOG

This list covers both the aircraft accidents and air raid incidents up to 1945 that occurred throughout Buckinghamshire which resulted in a loss of life or injury. It is not exhaustive.

| DATE | LOCATION | INCIDENT |
| --- | --- | --- |
| **1923** | | |
| 14 September | Ivinghoe | De Havilland DH34 G-EBBS. Crashed during heavy storm. 2 Crew and 3 Passengers killed. |
| **1939** | | |
| 28 April | Denham | Westland Lysander I. L4762. 13 Squadron. Aircraft crashed during conversion flight. Pilot killed. |
| **1940** | | |
| 7 August | North Crawley | Bristol Blenheim P4902. 17 OTU. Crashed in Rincroft Field, Mertlands Farm, North Crawley. Crew killed. |
| 10 August | Weston Turville | Miles Magister. N5431. HQ No.24 Group. Crashed at Weston Turville. Pilot killed. |
| 20 October | New Bradwell | Luftwaffe air raid on Wolverton. 5 civilians killed and 20 injured. |
| 15 November | Beachampton | Luftwaffe air raid hits Nash Road. 4 civilians killed. |
| 3 December | Milton Keynes | Airspeed Oxford I. L4642 & R6226. 14 SFTS. Two aircraft collided over Militon Keynes. 1 killed. |

# INCIDENT AND ACCIDENT LOG

| DATE | LOCATION | INCIDENT |
|---|---|---|
| **1941** | | |
| 17 March | Wolverton | Airspeed Oxford I. N4572. 14 SFTS. Aircraft crashed at Wolverton during night exercise flight. Crew killed. |
| 17 March | Bledlow | Hawker Hurricane I. Z7010. RAF Henlow. Dived into ground at Holly Green. ATA Pilot killed. |
| 18 November | Salford | Blenheim I L1353. 51 OTU. Aircraft struck a tree and crashed. Pilot & passenger killed. |
| 5 December | Piddington | Tiger Moth of 6 EFTS & Wellington I of 15 OTU collided in mid air. Pilots & crews killed. |
| **1942** | | |
| 3 July | Taplow | Miles Magister. R1889. 21 EFTS. Aircraft crashed on training flight. Pilot killed. |
| 8 August | Denham | A stick of 6 Luftwaffe bombs fell on Slough Trading Estate. 2 Policemen and 1 civilian killed. |
| 30 August | Cheddington | Wellington Ic DV825. 26 OTU. Crashed during training flight. Pilot injured. Navigator died from injuries. |
| 12 September | Wing | MB3 Prototype crashed during test flight. Company partner and test pilot, Valentine Henry Baker, killed. |
| 18 September | Aylesbury | Tiger Moth. T6821. 1 EFTS. Aircraft crashed during training flight. Pilot rescued. |
| 26 October | Langley | High expolsive bombs fell on Mead Avenue. 2 Civilians killed and 11 injured. |
| 6 November | Little Horwood | Wellington Ic DV885. 26 OTU. Crashed near airfield on training flight. 5 killed. |
| 11 December | Little Horwood | Wellington Ic X9622. 26 OTU. Crashed during night cross country training flight. Pilot & crew killed. |
| 22 December | Hoggeston | Wellington Ic ZB950 & DV915. 26 OTU. Aircraft collided in mid-air during training flight. Both crews killed. |

# INCIDENT AND ACCIDENT LOG

| DATE | LOCATION | INCIDENT |
|------|----------|----------|
| **1943** | | |
| 1 February | Beachampton Rectory | Wellington Ic X9755. 26 OTU. Crashed during training flight. Pilot & crew killed. |
| 15 March | Fawley | Halifax V DG283. 161 Squadron. Crashed on first leg of operational flight. 1 killed. |
| 11 April | Little Horwood | Vickers Wellington III. BJ879. 26 OTU. Aircraft struck Mursley Water Tower and crashed. Pilot & crew killed. |
| 8 June | East Claydon | Wellington III BJ833. 26 OTU. Crashed at Sionhill Farm during training flight. Pilot & crew killed. |
| 6 July | Little Horwood | Wellington III Z1664. 26 OTU. Aircraft made heavy landing. Pilot & crew injured. Gunner died of injuries. |
| 7 July | Wing | Wellington III X3955. 26 OTU. Crashed on take-off. Pilot & 2 crew members killed the remainder injured. |
| 7 August | Winslow | Wellington III X3790. 26 OTU. Overshot runway and crashed into village. 4 aircrew & 17 civilians killed. |
| 8 August | Wing | Wellington III BJ892. 26 OTU. Crashed on training flight with wreckage landing in Hertfordshire. Crew killed. |
| 13 November | Princess Risborough | B-17G 42-31038 GY:N 'Miriam'. 306 Bomb Group. Crashed on first leg of operational flight. Pilot killed. |
| 29 December | Finmere | Wellington X HE431. 16 OTU. Crashed on return from operational flight. Pilot & crew killed. |
| 30 December | Thornborough | Wellington III BK491. 26 OTU. Crashed at North End Farm during night training flight. Pilot & crew killed. |
| **1944** | | |
| 5 February | Fox Covert | Wellington X JA455. 26 OTU. Crashed on training flight due to loss of power. Pilot & crew killed. |
| 16 February | Gawcott | B-26 Mitchell. FL194. 13 OTU. Crashed during training flight. Dutch pilot & crew killed. |

# INCIDENT AND ACCIDENT LOG

| DATE | LOCATION | INCIDENT |
| --- | --- | --- |
| 23 February | Radnage | Messerschmitt Me 410A. 16/KG2. Shot down by Anti-Aircraft fire and crashed at Andridge Farm. Crew killed. |
| 14 March | Little Horwood | Vickers Wellington X HF480. 11 OTU. Crashed on return from operational flight. 4 killed. |
| 15 March | Quainton | Vickers Wellington X. LN660. 11 OTU. Collided with Stirling III EH989 of 90 Squadron. Both crews killed. |
| 24 March | Little Chalfont | Halifax III JD317. 1659 Heavy Conversion Unit. Shot down by friendly fire. Pilot & 3 crew killed, 3 survived. |
| 14 April | Foxcote | Mosquito NFII 13 OTU. Crashed on training flight. Pilot & crew killed. |
| 31 May | Westcott | Lancaster I. ME794. Crashed on return from operational flight. Pilot & crew survived. 1 ground personnel killed. |
| 9 June | Wing | Wellington X HE845. Crashed on airfield during training flight. Crew killed. 3 WAAFs on the ground killed. |
| 17 June | Wraysbury | V-1 exploded on Ouseley Road. 2 Civilians killed and 10 injured. |
| 2 July | Chesham Bois | V-1 shot down by Anti-Aircraft fire and landed in Chestnut Lane. 3 civilians killed and 17 injured. |
| 7 July | Wing | Wellington X LP314. 26 OTU. Crashed during training flight. Pilot & crew killed |
| 19 August | Iver | V-1 exploded at Love Hill House, Love Lane, Iver. One civilian killed. |
| 21 October | Kop Hill | C-47 Dakota crashed into top of hill during a supplies flight. Pilot & crew killed. |
| 15 November | Cheddington | B-24H Liberator. 36 Bomb Squadron. Crashed on take off in bad weather. Pilot & crew killed. |

# INCIDENT AND ACCIDENT LOG

| DATE | LOCATION | INCIDENT |
|---|---|---|
| **1945** | | |
| 3 January | Buckland | B-24H Liberator : 42-52650 'Cancer'. 406 Night Leaflet Squadron. Crashed on take-off. 3 killed. 3 injured. |
| 14 January | Wavendon | Mosquito II DD602. 51 OTU. Crashed whilst waiting for permission to land at Cranfield. Crew killed. |
| 11 February | Stoke Poges | V-2 struck the town causing damaged to property and some casualties. |
| 15 February | Iver Heath | V-2 exploded at Iver Heath. 17 injured. |
| 19 February | Cheddington | B-24H 42-50385 'Beast Of Bourbon'. 801st Bomb Squadron. Crashed during take-off. 3 killed & 3 injured. |
| 6 April | Winslow | Vickers Wellington X. HE928. & LN540. 26 OTU. Two aircraft collided in mid-air. Both crews killed. |
| 20 April | Taplow | Hudson V. AM854. Aircraft crashed during conversion training flight. ATA pilot & ATC cadet killed. |
| 30 April | Princess Risborough | Mosquito XII HK245. 51 OTU. Crashed on a GCI exercise flight. Pilot & crew killed. |
| **1950** | | |
| 15 February | Little Brickhill | De Havilland 108 Prototype. VW170. RAE. Crashed in high speed dive during test flight. Pilot killed. |

# SOURCES OF INFORMATION

## Archives

National Archives
 - Avia Series – Air Accident Investigation Reports
 - Air Series – Station & Operations Record Books
 - FO Series
 - HO Series
Bucks Herald Archives
Centre for Buckinghamshire Studies

## Websites

55th Fighter Group (www.55th.org)
Air Transport Auxiliary (www.poetryinaction-aviation.com/airtransportauxiliary )
American Battle Monuments Commission (www.abmc.gov)
Ancestry.com (http://www.cwgc.org)
Australian War Memorial (www.awm.gov.au)
Canadian Virtual War Memorial (http://www.veterans.gc.ca)
Commonwealth War Graves Commission (http://www.cwgc.org)
Findagrave.com (www.findagrave.com)
Findmypast.com (http://www.findmypast.co.uk)
Footnote.com (www.footnote.com)
London Gazette Archives (http://www.london-gazette.co.uk)
New Zealand Cenotaph Database (www.aucklandmuseum.com)
www.mackz.net

## My sincere thanks to the following for their assistance;

Debbi Bonas
Julian Evan-Hart
Celia Fulker (Martin-Baker Aircraft Company)
Andrew Gell
Susan Hartline
George Howe (Potton History Society)
Nigel Julian (56th Fighter Group Website)
Simon Parry
Mike Strange (Biggleswade History Society)
Ian White (305th Bomb Group Memorial Association)

*Buckinghamshire*

# REFERENCES

- Anderson, Christopher J. The Men of the Mighty Eighth: The U.S. 8th Air Force, 1942–1945 (2001). London. Greenhill

- Barnes, C.H. Bristol Aircraft Since 1910. (1970). London: Putnam

- Bishop, S & Hey, J. 8th Air Force Losses (Vol.1 – 3.) 1999. Cambridge. Bishop Book Productions

- Boiten, T. Bristol Blenheim. (1998) Marlborough, Wiltshire, UK: The Crowood Press.

- Bowman, Martin. 8th Air Force at War: Memories and Missions, England, 1942–1945. (1994) Cambridge. Patrick Stephens Ltd.

- Bowman, Martin. The Bedford Triangle. (1989) Cambridge. Patrick Stephens Ltd.

- Bowyer, C. Bristol Blenheim. (1984). London: Ian Allan.

- Bowyer, M J. Action Stations 6: Military Airfields of the Cotswolds and Central Midlands. (1989). Cambridge. Patrick Stephens Ltd.

- Chorley, W.R. RAF Bomber Command Losses of the Second World War: Volumes 1-9.(1998) Leicester, UK. Midland Publishing.

- Clark, F. Agents By Moonlight. (1999). Stroud. Tempus Publishing.

- Cull, B. Diver, Diver. (2008). London. Grub Street Publishing.

- Donald, W. John Burn One-Zero-Five. (2005). Peterborough. GMB Publishing.

- Freeman, Roger A. et al. The Mighty Eighth War Diary. (1981). London. Jane's Publishing Co.

- Fry, G L, Eagles Of Duxford. (1991). Shepperton. Ian Allan Publishing.

- Haining, P. The Flying Bomb War. (2002). London: Robson Books.

- Irons, R. Hitler's Terror Weapons: The Price of Vengeance. (2003). New York: HarperCollins.

- Jefford, C.G. RAF Squadrons. 2nd Edition. (2001) Shrewsbury, UK: Airlife Publishing.

- Mason, Francis K. The British Bomber Since 1914. (1994). London: Putnam Aeronautical Books.

- Maurer, Maurer. Air Force Combat Units of World War II. (1961, 1983). Office of Air Force History,

- McLaren, D. Beware The Thunderbolt. (1994). Pennsylvania. Schiffer Publications.

- Merrick, K A. Flights of the Forgotten. (1989). London. Arms & Armour Press

- Miller, Kent D. Fighter Units & Pilots of the 8th Air Force September 1942 – May 1945. (2000). Pennsylvania: Schiffer Publishing.

- O'Neil, B D. Half A Wing, Three Engines & A Prayer. (1999). Washington. McGraw-Hill Publishing.

- Ramsay, W. The Blitz Then & Now (Volume 3). (1990). London: Battle of Britain Prints International.

- Sharman, S. Sir Martin Baker. 1996. Yeovil. Patrick Stephens Publishing.

- Zaloga, S. V-1 Flying Bomb 1942–52. (2005). Oxford, UK: Osprey Publishing.